WALKING IN THE NATIONAL PARKS

WALKING IN THE
NATIONAL PARKS

ALAN MATTINGLY

Published in collaboration with
The Ramblers' Association

DAVID & CHARLES
Newton Abbot London North Pomfret (Vt)

British Library Cataloguing in Publication Data

Mattingly, Alan
  Walking in the national parks.
  1. National parks and reserves—England
  —Guide-books
  2. Walking—England
  I. Title II. Ramblers' Association
  914.2′04858 DA11

  ISBN 0–7153–8144–X

Photoset and printed in Great Britain
by Redwood Burn Limited, Trowbridge, Wiltshire
for David & Charles (Publishers) Limited
Brunel House Newton Abbot Devon

Published in the United States of America
by David & Charles Inc
North Pomfret Vermont 05053 USA

Contents

1
Introduction

The ten national parks of England and Wales were designated with the walker very much in mind. Indeed, several of the people involved in the designation process, which took place in the 1950s, were themselves keen ramblers. They were looking primarily for high, open country of outstanding scenic quality. Having selected the obvious areas – the Lakeland fells, the mountains of Snowdonia and the Dartmoor plateaux – they sought to draw the boundaries in such a way that these 'core' areas were surrounded, and in a sense protected, by a zone of lower country. This policy brought within the national parks, areas of woodland, farmland and valleys with sizeable villages and towns. The parks were therefore designed to offer walking of different kinds – long tough treks across remote fells, and shorter strolls along wooded riverbanks.

It is really only the walker who can appreciate the intricate and varied beauty of the national parks. And although the parks seem, on a modern road map, as if they are quite small and easy to reach (after all, it is now little more than a morning's drive from London to the Peak District), it can take a lifetime to appreciate the full richness of any one park. Some eminent people have dedicated their lives to their chosen national park – one thinks of Sylvia Sayer of Dartmoor, Arthur Raistrick of the Yorkshire Dales, and John Barrett of Pembrokeshire. Yet they still write with the same freshness and excitement that seizes the walker on his first day in a national park.

This book, then, is an introductory guide for walkers who are new, or relatively new, to our national parks. It seeks to fill a gap between those general guides that describe the geology, history and wildlife of the area but contain little practical information for walkers, and the detailed guides and maps that describe particular walks in a national park. It tries to help the walker in his choice of walks and publications, and it is designed to be of use when planning day walks, weekend trips or holidays of a couple of weeks.

A chapter is devoted to each national park and gives advice and information on: publications; public transport; long-distance paths in the park; short, waymarked trails; and guided walks. As appropriate, each chapter also gives advice on special dangers and weather conditions. There are, too, notes on rights of way and rights of access generally in the park. It is all very well telling the reader about the splendid ancient monuments and other historical features (which other guides do very well), but the walker wants to know how to get access to them so that they can be admired.

Some specific walks are suggested and these have been selected with walkers in mind who are new to a national park and who do not have a great deal of time on their hands. It is essential that a 1:50,000 or 1:25,000 Ordnance Survey map is taken along when one of these walks is tried. The route description offered should be of sufficient detail to allow it to be followed on the map, and then walked out on the ground.

As befits a book written for the Ramblers' Association, there are, interspersed throughout, comments on some of the disturbing things that are happening to national parks. The walker cannot fail to notice these and will be more sensitive to them than the motorist. There are military operations on Dartmoor, oil refineries in Pembrokeshire and conifer afforestation in the Cheviots. There is every reason to be bitter and complaining about some of these things, and no apology is offered for referring to them in this book. If we are to save national parks for those who love to walk in them, we have to be aware of the dangers and be prepared to help in overcoming them. With this theme in mind, the final chapter explores the future for national parks. It is a subject that all walkers should be keenly concerned about.

In the Appendix to the main chapters, a certain amount of background information is given. This includes details of addresses to write to for further information; the locations of national park information centres; and various publications of interest to the walker.

Please note that prices given were correct at the time of

writing – if necessary, readers should check them before setting out.

Finally, the reader will no doubt appreciate the quality of the photographs by Leonard and Marjorie Gayton that are spread throughout this book. I would like to thank the Gaytons most warmly for allowing their pictures to be reproduced here. I would also like to thank my colleagues at the Ramblers' Association, Cathy Brunsden and John Moore, for their work in bringing together much of the information contained in the Appendix and in other parts of the book, and Gwen Campbell for her assistance in typing the manuscript.

2
Dartmoor

The moorland plateau of Dartmoor is often thought of, and with some justice, as a formidable place. Several features combine to produce this impression – its remoteness from roads and settlements, its marshy terrain, its association with the prison, its mists, and its awesome granite tors which, with the many scattered megalithic monuments and abandoned buildings, make the land look utterly lonely and deserted.

For some people, this is enough to drive them to the more exquisite and beckoning country of Exmoor or Pembrokeshire. But for others, Dartmoor has a unique quality of wilderness which is to be treasured and guarded jealously. Sylvia Sayer, one of the foremost authorities on Dartmoor and also one of the country's most devoted and respected defenders of national parks, sums it up thus:

> Some regard Dartmoor simply as a barren waste, while others feel the magic of the place, perceiving that on Dartmoor's wild upland is written the history of the British race, and experiencing a sense of liberation and renewal whenever they set foot on it. They love its space and solitude, and the sound of the rivers that are Dartmoor itself with their lovely Celtic names – Dart, Tavy, Avon, Meavy, Ockment, Teign – rushing and cascading over their bouldered beds.
>
> Certainly wild country can be stern and austere and very testing, soaking the adventurous walker or rider to the skin, or freezing him to the marrow, reducing life almost to its barest elements. But something in human beings responds to this primeval toughness, and having surmounted it, feels enormously proud and benefitted by the experience.

The moor itself lies hard up against the park boundary at its northern and southern edges, but to the east and west, between the moorland edge and the park boundary, there is some delightful hill and valley country that, in the east in particular,

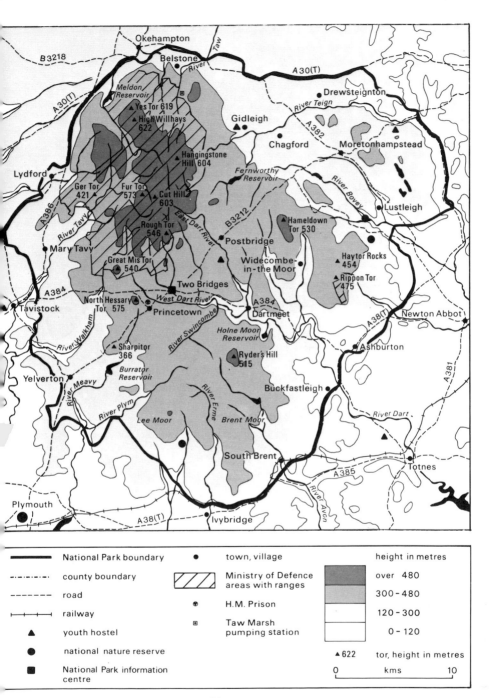

National Park boundary	town, village	height in metres
county boundary	Ministry of Defence areas with ranges	over 480
road	H.M. Prison	300 - 480
railway	Taw Marsh pumping station	120 - 300
youth hostel		0 - 120
national nature reserve		▲622 tor, height in metres
National Park information centre		0 kms 10

Hound Tor, from Hayne Down, near Manaton. On the left are Rippon Tor and Saddle Tor

offers walking country of a quite different nature. Here, there are extensive woodlands, deep incised valleys and moorland outliers.

It also has to be said that Dartmoor is not without its dull patches. The flat, unimposing country around Princetown and the prison, with its conifer plantations and TV mast, are best avoided or passed through quickly.

There are a number of guides which describe short walks (less than 10 miles) on Dartmoor (see Appendix) and the Forestry Commission has also laid out some short trails in its woods, notably near Lydford (just outside the national park and below the gorge itself); Fernworthy, near Chagford (with views over the reservoir below and the moors above); and at Bellever (with a particularly good walk leading up to Bellever Tor that commands fine views over the surrounding moors and valleys).

The national park committee runs the best programme of guided walks in any national park. In 1980 over 10,000 people took part. Walks are held on weekends throughout the year, and there is a fuller programme during the summer months. The walks vary in length, with the longest ones taking about 6 hours. They form an important part of the information service provided by the park authority, and as such are based on the idea that people can best learn about the moor by walking over it. With its wealth of ancient monuments and its fascinating wildlife, there is a lot to see. Part of the leader's job is to point out and explain features of interest. Some of the walks are of general interest, others are planned with particular interests in mind, such as botany, farming and history. There is a charge for taking part in the walks (£1 per adult on the 6-hour walks in 1980, for example), but no prior booking is required. Details of the walks and their starting points can be obtained from the national park office.

For the long-distance walker, the moor offers a real challenge. There are no official long-distance paths across the national park, but the RA's Two Moors Way runs from Ivybridge to Drewsteignton in the north, and thence across central Devon to Exmoor. The route avoids the northern moors and the highest part of the southern moors, but it provides an excellent traverse of the mixed country in the eastern part of the park, passing as it does through the most impressive stretches of the Dart and Teign valleys.

For those wishing to attempt the 'true' moorland crossing, keeping to the high ground as far as possible from Ivybridge to Okehampton, Hugh Westacott describes a 32-mile route in his booklet, as does Len Copley in *The Big Walks*. Copley's route actually starts at Belstone and is slightly to the east of Westacott's. It is marginally the more interesting and takes in more summits en route. However, both need to be prepared for and tackled with great care. An incident related by Len Copley on his north–south traverse illustrates very well the dangers of the moor. He describes how, just south of Ryder's Hill, 'disaster struck'. He continues:

> The ground in front, on either side and behind started to move, and we realised we were on a 'Quaker'. Being 'tail end Charlie' at this particular time, I was the one to break through the crust and sink up to my waist in slush (Quakers or Featherbeds occur when depressions in the granite fill with water and vegetation forms over the top, resulting in a deep stinking mass of rotting vegetation covered with a crust of bright green moss) . . .

The moor and the Teign valley, from Penhill

Copley was hauled out and the worst he seemed to suffer was the temporary distancing of himself from his companions until the smell wore off, but had he been on his own he would have been in some trouble.

John Hillaby *was* on his own when he had a similar misfortune on Dartmoor during his *Journey through Britain*. John, who more than makes up in writing skills what he clearly lacks in the art of navigation, also managed eventually to reach dry ground and continue on up to Land's End. But both incidents illustrate the fact that walking on the moor can have its surprises and that these are at best a nuisance and at worst a serious danger.

Mists too are something of a problem on Dartmoor. They roll in from the sea and can descend very quickly. A sudden mist can have a serious effect on one's sense of direction, and this emphasises the importance of careful map-reading at all times on Dartmoor and of ensuring that a compass is carried.

Mists and marshes may be a problem on Dartmoor, but they are not as great a cause of difficulty as getting around by public transport if you do not travel by car. The national park committee publishes a small booklet on summer bus services on the moor which also contains details of various special tickets that can be bought. The 'Moorbus Family Ticket', for example, gives unlimited travel for any group of up to two adults and two children for one day on six moorland bus services for £3. The authority also publishes a booklet of twenty or so short walks called *Bus away Walk-a-day*. Each walk has its starting and finishing point on a bus route, though cuts have reduced bus services since the booklet was published and walkers should check that the buses they need are still running.

The regular bus services are supplemented by a couple of mini-bus services running under the name of 'Pony Express'. One such service runs from Bovey Tracey to Widecombe and a second from Buckfastleigh to Postbridge. These buses stop at any point on the moor where it is safe to do so. Unfortunately, there is some doubt about their future, partly because of disappointing patronage.

There is a long tradition of free access on foot to the moors and, apart from the restrictions at firing times (see the notes on the northern moors below), walkers should not experience any difficulty in gaining access to open country in the national park. Much of the open land is common, and although this does not of itself confer a right of access, there has been de facto access on foot for as long as anyone can remember. Some open country is owned by the National Trust (such as Ringmoor Down in the south-west), and some is the subject of an access agreement (such as on Roborough Down, near Yelverton). Here, rights of access are doubly assured. In the valleys and the lower country there is a good network of paths that are maintained and signposted very well by the national park committee. Access to woodlands owned by the Forestry Commission and the National Trust is generally without restriction.

The northern moors

The northern moorland plateau, which rises to just over 2,000ft (610m) in the north-west (Yes Tor and High Willhays), is a unique English wilderness. The fearsome, lonely-looking granite tors are a source of wonder. They also provide good aids to navigation and obvious points to head for in planning a walk. But perhaps the most famous objective of all is Cranmere Pool, in the very centre of the wilderness. Actually, there is no 'pool' there today (although there is plenty of water above and below the surface in this area). Instead, walkers are often to be found heading for the 'letter-box' where they can leave a card or letter, stamp it with the distinctive rubber stamp and post it in the hope that the next person there will pick it up and post it on his or her return to civilisation. Since the Cranmere letterbox was started in the last century there have come into being over twenty such boxes throughout Dartmoor, each one maintained by a club, school or other organisation. The idea is, of course, quite daft, and has given rise to complaints from people who are worried about 'letterboxes' being embedded in old buildings and monuments on the moor and thereby damaging them.

Whether or not you stop at the Cranmere letterbox, the actual getting to it can be quite an effort. Eric Hemery describes a 13-mile circular route from Gidleigh to Cranmere and back in the official national park guide, and he lays

16

emphasis on the excellent views to be had en route from Hangingstone Hill, which 'marks the eastern limit of the Northern Morass' and from which Cranmere 'should not be attempted' if the weather is bad. You descend into the morass at your peril!

The routes from Gidleigh take you through marshy country – even by Dartmoor's standards. As an alternative, try an approach to Cranmere from the west, taking in the highest point of High Willhays on the return journey. The starting and finishing point is the dam on the Meldon reservoir. Follow the track alongside the eastern shoreline of the lake, and then follow the first tributary stream coming in from the south, traversing the slopes of this little valley all the way up to Black Tor. Stay parallel to the West Okement river and follow it deep into the moor, aiming for the torless summit of Great Kneeset, which overlooks the headwaters of the Okement and Tavy rivers.

Now head due east on a compass bearing across the great 'morass'. Having arrived at Cranmere Pool, keep to the highest ground by heading north to Okement Hill. High Willhays lies 2 miles away to the north-west – an hour's walk across wet plateau country. Before descending from High Willhays, walk over to Yes Tor from where, perched on the rocks, you will see the moor stretched out to the south and, to the north, the wooded margins of this vast wilderness. Head straight back to Meldon dam, being careful when picking your way across the rocky slopes below Yes Tor.

As you will find from this walk, there are few tracks and paths to guide you on your way across the northern moors. It is nearly all map and compass work. There are the occasional 'peat passes' providing useful routes through the deep peat – Hugh Westacott makes use of a couple of them across the heart of the moor on his transmoor crossing. Apart from these there are tracks used by the Services during their training on the moors – usually these are unsightly and out of place and in a few cases are actually metalled, providing a route for motor cars deep into the moorland plateau. In fact, Cranmere itself, remote as it appears to be, is within half a mile of one of these military roads. The roads detract greatly from the wild character of the national park. Although officially they are only private military roads, they are often open for and used by civilians in their cars. They should be closed or, even better, destroyed altogether at the earliest opportunity.

Unfortunately, virtually the whole of the northern moors is littered with the detritus of military activity – as well as the roads there are tatty look-out posts and flagpoles, tank tracks, shell craters in the moor, and shattered tors and monuments. It is a cause of great bitterness and anguish that the Services should be allowed to continue to misuse the national park as they do. But until such time as they are evicted, the walker has to put up with it. What you must ensure you do before going on to the northern moors – or at least into the 'Danger Areas' marked on the OS map – is to *find out if firing is taking place or not*. The warning flags are down on nearly all weekends and bank holidays, and continuously from mid-July to mid-September. Firing times are displayed in local newspapers, post offices and other public buildings. Information can be obtained by phoning Torquay 24592; Exeter 70164; Plymouth 701924; or Okehampton 2939.

The southern moors

South of Princetown and the River Dart lie the southern moors. These reach their highest point at Ryder's Hill (1,690ft, 515m). This is a rather dull summit which looks as if it is an outlier from the North Pennines and which is lacking in the unique features of the northern moors.

However, Ryder's Hill offers a good point to aim for in a day's walk. Such a walk could take in parts of two of the several tracks that are to be found on the southern moors. (In this respect, walkers are better served on the southern plateau than they are on the almost trackless 'Northern Morass'.) At Cross Furzes, 2 miles west of Buckfastleigh, the Abbot's Way can be picked up on the other side of the two-span clapper bridge over the Dean Burn ('one of the best bridges on the moor because of its situation and completeness', in the view of Brian Le Messurier). According to Eric Hemery, the title 'Abbot's Way' is a romanticised name for a wool jobbers' track used in the Middle Ages. The true Abbot's Way, he says, is marked by thirteen medieval stones and follows an easier route across the southern

18

moors between today's Burrator and Venford reservoirs via Nun's Cross Farm. (See *The Great Outdoors*, March 1981.)

The misnamed Abbot's Way shown on the OS maps is itself discontinuous, although with a little compass work its remnants can be followed across the moor from the Avon valley into that of the River Plym at Plym Steps. However, from Cross Furzes it offers an intermittent route across the moor, north of the Avon reservoir to another, smaller but more remote clapper bridge. From here, it is a long plod up to the summit of Ryder's Hill. To return to Buckfastleigh, head north and pick up the Sandy Way, another track which traverses the moor, this time from Foxtor Mires to Holne.

A track of a very different nature is the 'Redlake tramway'. This runs from near Ivybridge to the disused Redlake china-clay works, almost along the spine of Ugborough Moor. The tramway was built in 1910 and the lines were removed in 1932. Today it offers a natural walking route into the southern moors, and the views to the south across Devon and the English Channel are magnificent – among the best in the park. For example, start at Ivybridge, climb up on to the tramway and follow it as far as the summit marked by Petre's Cross. Then head east to White Barrows and follow this line of high ground across Brent Moor and down to Shipley Bridge. From here, you can follow country lanes and paths to South Brent.

The eastern moors

The most visited moors lie north of the River Dart and south-east of the Two Bridges–Moretonhampstead road. The renowned village of Widecombe-in-the-Moor sits snugly in the middle.

In many ways, this area offers more interesting country to walk in than the vast northern and southern plateaux. The tors are fantastic and gigantic. Hound Tor, Haytor Rocks, Rippon Tor and the rest loom over the surrounding country in an awe-inspiring way. Walks in this area can be planned to take in many types of country – the open moor and the tors, the gorse-covered commons below the high ground, and the deep wooded valleys. There is a profusion of ancient monuments (notably the wonderfully preserved ancient settlement of

Widecombe, from Chinkwell Tor

Grimspound) and a number of outstandingly attractive villages and hamlets, such as Widecombe and Ponsworthy (both best visited out of season). The scope for planning varied walks in this area is endless.

For instance, a round trip of about 13 miles that takes in many of the prominent features of this area starts at Widecombe itself and follows paths on to the long moorland ridge to the west of the village which, as you walk northwards, leads to Hameldown Beacon and Hameldown Tor. This is the highest point on the walk and the views around are marvellous, but the best is yet to come. Descend a short distance to admire the camp at Grimspound and then follow a bridleway eastwards across the main ridge and around the head of the Webburn valley right the way across to Hound Tor. Although you are barely above 1,000ft (305m), the view from this perched, rocky eminence on the edge of the moorland is absolutely splendid. The deep wooded valley of the River Bovey lies below and the rounded hills on either side of the Teign valley are beyond.

There is a well-worn path from Hound Tor across the little wooded valley to the east and up on to Haytor Down, from where you head south to Haytor Rocks themselves. Despite the litter and the crowds, these rocks never fail to inspire wonder and amazement at the geological forms that nature can devise.

After stopping for a while at Haytor, head south-west across the moor past Saddle Tor to Rippon Tor for a view over the hills and valleys that lie behind the coastal resorts around Tor Bay. Finally, head north-west across open country to pick up a country lane leading back to the starting point in Widecombe.

The western margins

Tucked in between the moor and the edge of the national park is some fine country on the western margins of Dartmoor. The stunning gorge of Lydford and the church on Brent Tor are well worth visiting as part of a walk that takes in the north-western edges of the moor and the valleys that run off it.

For instance, park near Brent Tor and, after visiting the church, follow a bridleway and a country lane eastwards into the valley at Wortha Mill Bridge. Then start a long steady climb on to open country, heading for the top of Gibbet Hill, an isolated summit overlooking the broad Tavy valley below. Next, keep to the ridge heading north-east towards Willsworthy Camp; follow the line of the A386 for a short distance and then descend by a farm track that runs under a disused railway into the village of Lydford. At the south end of the village, access can be gained to the stunning ravine of Lydford Gorge. After leaving the gorge at its southern end, follow tracks and paths down the valley to North Brentor, and then keep to country lanes for the last mile to regain Brent Tor.

Further south, Roborough Down and the country around Horrabridge rewards slight effort with views over the valleys and lower country to the south and west. Roborough Down itself is covered by an access agreement and is a long expanse of open common that is exhilarating to walk over.

Burrator reservoir is thought by some to be attractive, and many people go for short walks along the road that encircles it or via the forest tracks that overlook it. However, a higher recommendation can be given to the Plym valley, reached from Burrator by a brisk walk over Ringmoor Down. The upper part of the valley is open country covered with enclosures and hut circles. Lower down, below Cadover Bridge, there is a beautiful walk along the 'Pipe Track' (after a pipe that brought china-clay material down from the moors to what are now the remains of a china-clay drying plant at Shaugh Bridge). This track passes through some lovely woodlands and at its lower end, overlooks the Dewerstone, a granite cliff nearly 200ft (61m) high.

The Dart, the Bovey and the Teign

The Dart valley below the honeypot of Dartmeet is deep, wooded and very beautiful. There are paths and tracks through some of the woods (the National Trust owns part of the land), but the valley is perhaps best viewed from the tors that overlook it – notably Sharp Tor and Combestone Tor.

Combestone Tor can be reached in a half hour or so by following the bridleway leading up from Dartmeet, and the walk out and back to this point makes for a very agreeable short stroll. For a longer walk with a succession of fine views across the Dart valley and its tributaries, start at New Bridge where the B3357 crosses the River Dart, and then follow the river downstream for a mile or so, keeping off the roads where possible. Then turn up on to higher ground aiming for Spitchwick Manor. Take the right of way that leads to Leusdon Church and then follow a country lane to the village of Ponsworthy. From here, you can soon gain open country and walk to the top of the 1,400ft (427m) hill crowned by Corndon Tor. It is then nearly all downhill, with Mel Tor to the south-east the next objective. After this point you follow Dr Blackall's drive – a specially designed scenic drive of Victorian origin, which is possibly the earliest on record! The drive takes you to Aish Tor, overlooking the great incised meander in the River Dart below, and from here there is a sharp descent back to New Bridge.

It is in this area – where the views extend across the open moor, down into the rich lowlands of Devon and below into the steep valley of the Dart – that some of the best short walks on Dartmoor are to be enjoyed.

The valley of the River Bovey, further north, is generally much wider and less engaging than that of the Dart. However, near Lustleigh the Bovey passes through a narrow stretch, and here there is once again some very fine hill and valley country. From Lustleigh it is a stiff but rewarding climb up to the viewpoints of Sharpitor and Hunter's Tor. From here, Hound Tor and the eastern moors stand out in very commanding fashion. From Sharpitor, a descent into the Bovey valley and a walk back to Lustleigh through the woods provides rapid changes of scene in a short distance.

Most dramatic of all is the River Teign, between Hunter's Tor and Steps Bridge. Here, the river passes through a valley – a gorge almost – which is overhung by rock faces and oak and conifer woods. The area could qualify as a miniature national park in its own right. It is utterly different, and indeed detached from, the rest of the national park, but a walk in this area should be a high priority for anyone spending a few days on Dartmoor. The classic route is from Castle Drogo (a twentieth-century creation now owned by the National Trust), down into the valley and along the Fishermen's Path to Fingle

Fingle Bridge, on the River Teign

Bridge, and then back on the higher route of the Hunters' Path.

From Fingle Bridge there are paths all the way downriver to Steps Bridge, and although this is a very pleasant walk, it is better to devise a route that takes in some of the higher ground to the north or south. Drewsteignton to the north and Chagford to the west offer good starting and finishing points for walks in this part of the national park (Chagford can be reached by riverside footpaths from Hunter's Tor).

3
Exmoor

The Exmoor National Park has three great attractions for walkers – its high expanse of grass and heather moor, its stunning coastline, and its deep, winding, wooded valleys. Looked at as a whole, the park can be seen as a wild and romantic hunting ground, or as a delicate flower whose fragile beauty is threatened by a growing invasion of cars and caravans and the creeping uniformity of modern agriculture. It is still for all that a majestic area in which to ramble, and is one that has a particular appeal for those who find the interminable marshy plateaux of Dartmoor and the Pennines to be a little tedious sometimes. For Exmoor is full of variety and colour, and the scene changes rapidly as you move along.

The national park can be traversed on foot along two long-distance paths. The South West Peninsula Coast Path (South West Way) runs along (and often high above) the coastline from east to west; and the RA's Two Moors Way crosses the southern boundary of the national park near West Anstey and heads north across moors and valleys to terminate at Lynmouth.

Thirty-five miles of the South West Way run along the national park coastline, from Minehead to Combe Martin. Exmoor shares with the North York Moors the sudden and remarkable conjunction of high moorland and coastline, and this stretch of the Way is, in parts, as much of a moorland walk as a coastal one. The cliffs are, of course, high and dramatic; there is a multitude of sandy, rock-girt bays (often inaccessible); and there are any number of steep-sided combes with streams running swiftly through woods and open country down to the sea.

The walk can be accomplished with no hardship in a weekend. For convenient stop-over points, aim to arrive at Minehead by early afternoon so that you can reach Porlock on the first night. Head next day for Lynmouth and you will be in

25

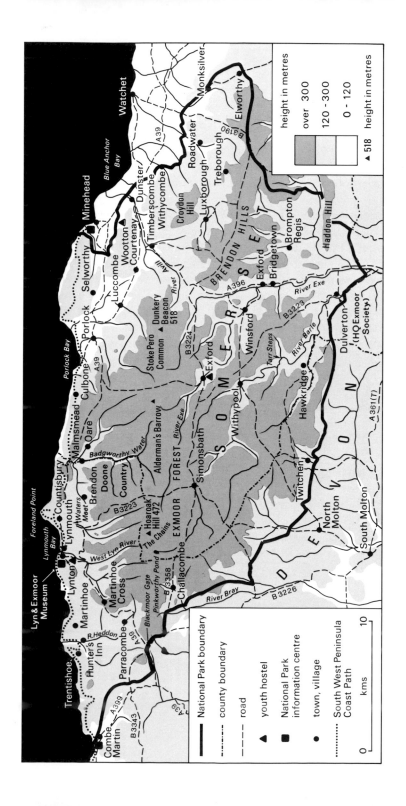

Combe Martin well before evening on the third day, in time to catch a bus home.

The route runs at a high level partly because of the difficulty of access to the shoreline – actually, to see most of the coast you have to take a boat! Thus the path starts at Minehead and immediately climbs high up on to the top of North Hill and runs close to the summit of Selworthy Beacon, giving a superb view across the coast to South Wales and inland to the heart of the moor. On the other side of Porlock Bay, the path climbs up through woodland and then contours along a track through farmland at a height of nearly 1,000ft (305m), emerging on the coast road at County Gate. On the other side of Lynmouth, the path climbs high above the appropriately named Woody Bay and then follows the old coast road to Hunter's Inn, which lies in one of the deepest and most strikingly beautiful valleys in the national park. The Way then regains its upland character by making for the summits of Holdstone Down and Great Hangman before descending to Combe Martin.

The Two Moors Way provides an excellent 26-mile route for walkers seeking to make their first acquaintance with the inland parts of the national park. Spread over two days, the journey can be conveniently broken at Simonsbath, in the heart of the moor.

From West Anstey to Exe Head the Way runs across the 'grain' of the country. It first crosses the long southern ridge that runs from Challacombe in the west to Dulverton. (This ridge, incidentally, provides the longest and one of the most splendid high-level walking routes in the national park. It commands very extensive views across the rich mid-Devon farmland to Dartmoor in the south. Unfortunately, it is followed along almost its entire length by a metalled country road, but in mid-week out of season there is very little traffic running along it.)

The Way then descends into the Barle valley at the famous Tarr Steps (an ancient clapper bridge). It follows this sublimely beautiful valley upstream – first alongside the river through the delightful woodlands, and then across the slopes overlooking the valley to a point 1½ miles west of Simonsbath. After climbing up to Exe Head, the Way descends rapidly into the valleys of the East Lyn and its tributaries, leaving behind it

Combe Martin Bay and the Hangman Hills

another smooth moorland ridge, known as The Chains. The final stretch stays above the Lyn valley and rewards the walker with grand views across to Countisbury Common and the sea beyond.

What can't be gleaned from books on Exmoor (see Appendix) can often be learnt from the OS 1in Tourist Map. This depicts public rights of way (600 miles of them altogether, and many of them waymarked by the national park office), major viewpoints, National Trust land and other features. There is normally unrestricted access on foot to National Trust land, and fortunately the Trust owns large tracts of glorious hill and coastal country around Bossington Hill (overlooking Porlock Bay), Dunkery Beacon (the highest point in the national park at 1,700ft [518m]), Winsford Hill, the Heddon valley and elsewhere.

There is also a long tradition of public access to the open moorland and heathland of the national park. Very occasionally 'Keep Out' notices are seen, but the main problem is that over the years, much open country has been converted to forestry plantations and enclosed 'improved' pasture. This conversion to agricultural land destroys the open, semi-natural character of the moor and eliminates de facto access at the same time. Although on a wet and windy day the uplands of the national park may appear wild and barren, the soils and climate of Exmoor are more favourable for farming than those on the moors and fells of northern England, and it is well within the capacity of modern agricultural technology to tame and enclose most of the remaining open country. The loss of an estimated 12,300 acres of Exmoor's open country since World War II has become the subject of nationwide concern among conservationists. It is an issue that is discussed at more length in Chapter 12.

The Exmoor National Park Committee was one of the first to provide waymarked trails and they now start at over twenty

Bossington and Porlock Bay, from Bossington Hill on the National Trust's Holnicote Estate

different locations in the park. There are also nature trails, and the national park office has devised an ambitious and varied programme of guided walks. These vary in length from 2 to 10 miles, and there is a charge of 50p per person (free for children). There are two types of walks – general walks, for which there is no need to book in advance and special-interest walks, for which places should be reserved in advance by phoning Dulverton 23665. The general walks start at several different places in the park, and the special-interest walks include walks at dawn ('dawn on Exmoor is special', the park office says – provided you can get to the starting point by 5.00am), and walks which pay particular attention to bird watching and archaeology. There is also a guided walk around Wimbleball lake – this is a large new reservoir located in the southern part of the national park below Haddon Hill. The walks are held from April to September each year, and the details are set out in a free leaflet which is available from the national park office.

There is no hiding the fact that it is not easy to travel around Exmoor by public transport. There are no rail links to the national park, although the once-closed line to Minehead has been opened for restricted services by a private company. From June to September there is a special bus service along the coast road between Ilfracombe and Watchet, and this is very handy when you want to walk along a section of the South West Way and return by public transport to the point you started from. But, outside the coastal zone, bus services are very patchy. For further details of this service contact the national park office or write to the main service operator – Western National Omnibus Co Ltd, National House, Queen Street, Exeter.

The Brendon Hills

East of the A396, running southwards from Dunster, is a range of hills known as the Brendons, which rises to nearly 1,400ft (427m) at Lype Hill. Although this was once an area of extensive heathland, there is now very little open country left, and the land is cultivated or, as on the northern slopes, covered with conifer plantations. Nevertheless, there are still some very attractive walks to be had in this part of the national park, with fine views from the high ground across the Bristol Channel and the open moors to the west.

For a walk which takes in some of these views, start at Dunster and follow the waymarked path for Withycombe through the woods of Dunster Park. Head for the top of Withycombe Hill, from where there is a good view over the coastal plain below. Then head southwards along Stapling Lane towards Withycombe Common, which, although surrounded by forests, is open at the top. There is then a sharp descent to Kingsbridge, nestling in a quiet valley, and from here you can follow a waymarked trail past Newcombe Farm and Colley Hill to the top of Lype Hill itself. Here is the last remaining outlier of heathland on the main Brendon ridge. The waymarked path then takes you down to Wheddon Cross (which is on the main road) along a track that skirts around the top of the steep wooded valleys running off to the north.

The coastal zone

At the far eastern end of Exmoor's coastal zone stands a superb isolated block of upland, lying between Porlock and Minehead. One could spend an entire day up here, exploring the coves and woodlands and admiring the extensive views across the Bristol Channel and Exmoor. However, for a walk of 6 or 7 miles that takes in the best features of this area, follow the coast road to the picture-postcard village of Selworthy, climb through the woods and head for Bossington Hill, overlooking the western scarp of this block of hills. Then turn back eastwards along the crest of the hill past Selworthy Beacon and North Hill, descending along the coast path to Minehead.

Over to the west, the East Lyn river runs in a deep narrow valley parallel to the coastline. A walk along the coast path between County Gate and Lynmouth (and preferably in that direction, since the latter point is 1,000ft (305m) lower than the former) is particularly to be recommended for its views. In its early stages these are across the East Lyn valley and later, as the path runs towards Foreland Point and up to Countisbury Common, there is a great panorama of the West Somerset and North Devon coastline.

Between Lynmouth and Combe Martin, the coastline dips
and rises and, as in the Valley of Rocks, assumes some fantastic
shapes. The Heddon valley cuts particularly deeply into the
high ground bordering the coastline. To sample some of this
dramatic and (as it must have seemed to past generations)
mysterious landscape, start at Hunter's Inn and walk down the
valley to the sea at Heddon's Mouth. Scree-covered slopes soar
above this narrow, unspoilt valley. The screes can be scaled at
one or two points, but there is nothing lost in returning all the
way to Hunter's Inn before beginning the next stage of the
walk. This is back to Lynmouth along the coast path, which
first climbs steadily to the Roman signal station in the Valley of
Rocks and Lynmouth beyond.

The eastern moors and valleys

The principal attractions of this area – defined roughly as that
part of the park lying south of the coastal zone, west of the
A396 and east of a line running north–south through Exford
and Withypool – are the heather- and bracken-clad hills of
Dunkery and Winsford; the sylvan glades of the Barle valley
between Dulverton and Withypool; and the extensive and very
beautiful National Trust woodlands in the Horner valley and
above Luccombe.

Two full-day walks of around 15 miles each can be strongly
recommended for experiencing the main splendours of this
part of the national park. The first starts way over in the village
of Dunster, just off the main coast road. Climb on to the high
ground to the west of Dunster, not failing to turn round on
gaining the ridge to catch what is the most striking view of this
famous Exmoor village. Follow the ridge along into the
forestry plantations and keep to it until just past the trig point,
then take the track that descends to the idyllic village of
Wootton Courtenay. From here, follow the road to Brockwell
and pick up the path which leads on to open country and
climbs steadily up the broad eastern shoulder of Dunkery Hill.
The beacon is reached just beyond the road and the view from
here, although one of the most extensive in the national park, is
essentially that of a view from the edge of the moor. To the
north, east and south are the sea, the woods, the valleys and the

farmland. But to the west is the moor, stretching as far as the horizon.

Head due west along the broad summit of the park's highest ridge to Rowbarrows. Start the descent by aiming north–west around the head of Lang Combe and then north along the ridge to the west of the combe, parallel to the motor road. At the end of the open country, follow the road for a short while until it crosses Horner Water. Then turn right into the woods and follow the path that runs close by the river all the way round to Horner. This is as fine a woodland walk as can be had anywhere in England, and it is full of interest for bird-watchers and naturalists. The final stretch of the walk is from Horner to Porlock on the main coast road, from where a bus can be taken back to Dunster. You can either follow a low-level route, along a woodland path and then a country road around the foot of Crawter Hill, or if you have the energy left, climb through the woods to the open top of the hill itself before descending to

The River Barle at Landacre Bridge

Porlock. The view across the woods below and Porlock Bay with the coastal hills on either side will more than reward the effort.

The second walk starts and finishes at Dulverton and takes in Winsford Hill, Tarr Steps and the Barle valley. Head due north out of Dulverton along a track running parallel to the B3223 towards Court Down. This meets a metalled lane which should be followed for a mile or so on to the next ridge at a place called Summerway. From here there is a bridleway route to Winsford, which begins by descending into a steep combe planted with conifers. Winsford is another Exmoor village worth lingering in. Take the road climbing westwards out of Winsford and then follow the path that leads off from it to Withycombe at the foot of a deep valley known as the Punchbowl. The waymarked path curves round the western slopes of the Punchbowl to the summit of Winsford Hill itself. From here you can see far into the deep valleys of the Exe and the Barle, that run north-westwards into the heart of the moor.

Follow the line of the B3223 for a while, then turn off to the left along a track that descends sharply into the wooded Barle valley past Great Bradley. Follow the path along the eastern bank of the river through attractive woodlands all the way to Tarr Steps. At Tarr Steps, cross the river and follow the road opposite up to Hawkridge. From here there is a track leading south-eastwards along the splendid route of Hawkridge ridge, with high-level views across the Barle valley. This track eventually descends into the woodlands once again and joins the river just opposite the tree-covered mound of Mounsey Castle. A path on the south bank of the river leads all the way back to Dulverton.

The western moors and valleys

This central 'core' of Exmoor, lying west of Exford and south of the coastal zone, largely consists of the ancient hunting territory of Exmoor Forest. Much of it is of a wild and austere character, but for the rambler it is prime hill-walking country.

The main ridge is that of The Chains. These grass-covered moors are sometimes wet and tussocky, and no walker should underestimate the amount of effort needed to cross them. For a

walk that takes in most of the ridge, start at or close by Parracombe, cross the main road opposite Churchtown and follow
the track which takes you on to the metalled road running
along the top of Parracombe Common. Follow this towards
Chapman Barrows, at the western end of the main ridge. From
here, there are nearly 4 miles of tough moorland walking, eastwards along the line of the high ground to the col of Exe Head.
At this point, turn left along a track descending into the valley
of Hoaroak Water. The walk now follows the route of the Two
Moors Way back to Lynmouth. The track climbs on to Furze-
hill Common, and you keep to this ridge to emerge at Stock
Common. Here, turn right and follow tracks and lanes through
Cheriton to Hillsford. Follow the A39 towards Lynton for a
short distance and then take the track along the upper slopes of
the valley marked 'footpath to Lynmouth'.

Every Exmoor walker will also want to walk through 'Doone
country'. A recommended walk starts at County Gate on the
A39 and immediately descends steeply to the tourist honeypot
of Malmsmead at the foot of the Badgworthy valley. There is a
very well-marked track leading up the valley alongside the
river. The surrounding country becomes increasingly more
open and wild – the day-trippers tend to thin out pretty quickly
as well. You emerge at the head of Badgworthy Water into a
huge moorland basin with tributary valleys coming in from all
sides. The ground around here can be very marshy, so it is best
to keep to the track that leads eastwards uphill past the
deserted outpost of Larkbarrow until, at long last, a hill road is
reached at Alderman's Barrow. To return to the coast road at a
convenient point, head north-east towards Lucott Moor and
follow the long ridge that winds round to the north of the
Horner Water valley and brings you out at the excellent viewpoint on Ley Hill, overlooking Porlock just below.

There are a great many other fine walks to be had in this
heartland of Exmoor. But if time is short, make sure that you
spend half a day exploring the Barle valley immediately below
Simonsbath. The valley here is open and rough in places, but
it is a sheltered, intimate landscape which is ideal for riverside
picnics on a sunny day. There is a track along the eastern bank
of the river leading out of Simonsbath, and this takes you down
to the steep-sided mound of Cow Castle where the White

Water valley flows in from the north. This is an ideal place for lingering in on a hot summer's day. To return to Simonsbath, wander up the White Water valley for a short distance and then pick up a track at Picked Stones which climbs up on to a ridge, goes past Winstitchen Farm and descends to the starting point.

4

The Peak District

With the possible exception of Northumberland, it is more difficult to comprehend the Peak District as a single entity than almost any other national park. The Lake District has its radial pattern of lakes and glaciated valleys; Dartmoor and Exmoor have their central cores of moorland; Pembrokeshire is almost entirely coastline scenery. But the Peak District contains such an astonishing variety of landscape that no one feature can be said to typify the national park.

In the north there is Black Hill, a bare morass of wet peat relieved only by the white triangulation point sitting apologetically on what the surveyors from Southampton claim is the highest point. Thirty-five miles to the south and 1,500ft (457m) below is Dovedale, a deep limestone valley rich in colour, vegetation and absurd place-names such as Jacob's Ladder and Lover's Leap. To the west are the bizarre outcrops of rocks, The Roaches and Hen Cloud, and to the east is the wide, fertile valley of the Derwent, with Chatsworth House standing in a majestic parkland setting.

In fact, the park is held together as a unity not so much by what lies within its boundaries as by what lies outside. For just over the borders are millions of people and hundreds of square miles of industry and development. The Peak is nothing if not popular, and while it is still possible to find solitude on the hills if you know when to go and where, the experience of walking in the Peak is best enjoyed by those who don't expect to be alone and who know the value of a friendly 'how-do' every half hour or so.

Moreover, being in the position that it is, the Peak has not exactly escaped the attentions of the road builders, the water boards and the mineral extractors. Far from it – a lot of damage has been done and the newcomer to the Peak District National Park should not expect to find the landscape in an unmolested

37

state. Indeed, the Peak is continually under pressure. At the time of writing, for example, the northernmost valley, Longdendale, is being considered as a site for a vast new hydro-electric project, with roads, pipelines, a new reservoir on the moors and constantly fluctuating water levels in the reservoir lakes below. An unwelcome intrusion if ever there was one.

But although the struggle to protect the beauty and tranquillity of the Peak continues, at least the main battles for *access* to the moors of the national park have been fought and won. The Peak District was, of course, the scene of the 'mass trespass' of the 1930s – vividly recalled by Howard Hill in his book *Freedom to Roam*. Most of the northern and eastern hills are now covered by access agreements, under which ramblers are given the 'right to roam' (except for a few days during the shooting season) and the landowners are paid handsome compensation in return. On the western and eastern flanks of the park, where to wander away from the path is still to commit an act of trespass, walkers are unlikely to be turned back from the open moor, even if they are trespassing. Anyone who is unfortunate enough to be told to leave should inform the Ramblers' Association. If the situation warrants it, we shall bring pressure to bear to try and have access restored. This is exactly what happened in the case of The Roaches where, with strong backing from the RA, the Peak Park Board purchased the land in order to ensure that people could continue to walk across it without hindrance.

There is a good network of paths throughout the national park and, by and large, they are in good condition. The network of public rights of way is supplemented by special trails along disused railway lines that have been acquired by the Peak Park Board (notably the Tissington Trail and the High Peak Trail, which are both in the southern part of the park), and by informal 'concessionary' paths in certain areas, such as in Chatsworth Park and around Castleton. (As it happens, the Castleton concessionary paths are the subject of some controversy, because the RA claims that the rights of way which the concessionary paths in this area are supposed to supplement are being deliberately neglected.)

By rural standards, public transport in the park is excellent.

Dovedale, near Dove Holes

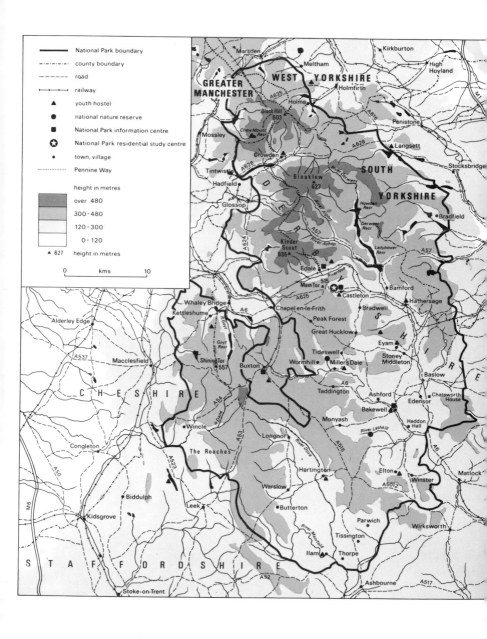

Legend

National Park boundary
county boundary
road
railway
▲ youth hostel
● national nature reserve
■ National Park information centre
✪ National Park residential study centre
· town, village
···· Pennine Way

height in metres
over 480
300 - 480
120 - 300
0 - 120
▲ 627 height in metres

0   kms   10

Marsden
Kirkburton
Meltham
High Hoyland
WEST YORKSHIRE
GREATER MANCHESTER
A635
Holmfirth
Holme
Black Hill 603
A616
Penistone
Mossley
Chew Moor Resr
Crowden
A628
Langsett
Tintwistle
A628
Stocksbridge
Hadfield
SOUTH
Bleaklow 627
River Derwent
YORKSHIRE
Glossop
Howden Resr
Bradfield
A624
A57
Derwent Resr
River Ashop
Kinder Scout 835
River Noe
Ladybower Resr
A57
Edale 515
Mam Tor
Castleton
Bamford
Hathersage
Whaley Bridge
Chapel-en-le-Frith
Bradwell
Kettleshume
A6
Peak Forest
Great Hucklow
Eyam
Alderley Edge
R. Goyt
Goyt Resr
Tideswell
Stoney Middleton
A537
Shining Tor 557
Buxton
Wormhill
Miller's Dale
Baslow
Macclesfield
CHESHIRE
A6
Ashford
Edensor
Chatsworth House
Taddington
Bakewell
Haddon Hall
A54
Monyash
River Lathkill
Wincle
River Wye
Longnor
A6
Congleton
The Roaches
Hartington
River Dove
Elton
Winster
Matlock
A50
A523
Warslow
A5012
M6
Biddulph
Leek
Butterton
Parwich
Wirksworth
Kidsgrove
River Manifold
Tissington
STAFFORDSHIRE
Ilam
Thorpe
A52
Ashbourne
A517
Stoke-on-Trent

The Manchester–Sheffield railway line through Edale is an excellent facility for walkers, taking them from the centre of these cities to the heart of the national park in a very short time. Bus services are likewise good, with express services running between the cities surrounding the park, a number of regular local services, and extra weekend buses sponsored by the Peak Board itself. The board publishes a comprehensive set of timetables for buses in the Peak.

The park is full of historical and archaeological interest, and two aspects of this heritage deserve special mention. A number of rights of way follow old drove roads and green lanes, many of which have a long and engrossing history. A second fascinating subject is the lead mining industry – or rather, the remains of it. Mineshafts and old workings litter the 'White Peak' – the southern, limestone part of the park. Apart from their historic and geological interest, however, these old workings also have their dangers. People have been killed and injured by falling down old shafts, and a Code of Practice has been published in which walkers are exhorted to keep to the paths and watch out for warning signs. But beware – not all old shafts have been located and signposted. Whenever you approach hummocky ground in the limestone country go very carefully and, above all, don't let young children and animals run around in these areas.

If you prefer shorter walks, there are two easy waymarked walks in Forestry Commission land near the Errwood reservoir in the Goyt valley (south of Whaley Bridge) and near the Snake Pass (starting at the Birchenclough lay-by on the A57). There are also a number of published guides describing short walks in the Peak, including several excellent ones produced by the Peak Board itself.

For those who have much more energy and relish a challenge, there is the famous southern section of the Pennine Way, from Edale to Marsden. This, the most testing and daunting section of the whole 250-mile route, is described by Roger Redfern in *The Big Walks* as 'unquestionably the most famous moorland traverse in the Peak District, the great classic of the Southern Pennines by which all other long walks in the area are judged'. Other long-distance walks (unofficial ones, this time) include John Merrill's Peakland Way, a 96-mile circular walk around the national park, and the Gritstone Way, a route from Derby to Edale along the eastern gritstone edges that was planned by members of the Derby Group of the RA. Walkers who finish the Gritstone Way with a day or two to spare have the option of picking up the 40-mile Derwent Watershed Walk at Edale and following this route (also described in *The Big Walks*) around the headwaters of the Derwent and its tributaries. As the following notes on the northern moors imply, such a walk is extremely demanding, both in terms of energy and time. The 'Dark Peak' is landscape that you have to be patient with – the black moors seem to go on for ever and take time to reveal the many glorious views that they have to offer.

Black Hill and Longdendale

There is no doubt that Longdendale would be much better off without its reservoirs and power-lines, but the scenery in the valley is not so bad as is frequently made out. The park board have plans for improving some of the paths, and with the publication of David Frith's *Pathwise in Glossop and Longdendale*, ramblers now have an excellent written description of possibilities for walking in this area. Frith's book is particularly commendable because he shows by meticulous description and historical reference how fascinating even the most unobtrusive footpath can be. Moreover, he doesn't shrink from identifying unco-operative farmers and ineffective local authorities – something to which other writers of walking guides might devote more space.

However, if reservoirs and power-lines aren't your idea of good scenery, you can quickly escape from Longdendale by following one of the many paths that lead off to the north or south. But be warned – the walking here is not for the unwary. It is vital that map and compass are carried and that you know how to make good use of them. Proper walking boots are absolutely essential. In fact, if you venture on to the moors north of Longdendale you would be very lucky, even on a dry summer's day, to return to the valley without having thoroughly muddied your boots and having needed on at least one occasion to take a compass bearing.

Black Hill itself is the obvious point to aim for. The easiest route is from the east, where the A6024 climbs to over 1,700ft (518m) and offers a starting point for a short, if boggy, walk to Black Hill from near the Holme Moss television station. From the west, the obvious route is up the deep valley of Chew Brook, past Chew reservoir and through a pass over the moors, to join the Pennine Way en route for the summit. But perhaps the best ascent is from Crowden in Longdendale. A good circular route begins here and climbs around the western side of the Loftend quarry to gain the ridge that takes the walker on to the spongy moor of Hey Moss and then up to Westend Moss and White Low. From here there is a long trek up to Black Hill itself, with the last half mile or so across a dark marshy morass which defies anyone to keep to a straight line for the top.

For the return journey, come back along the clearly marked Pennine Way. The great surprise of this part of the walk is to be taken by the Way along the top of Laddow Rocks, from where there is a spectacular view down the valley of Crowden Great Brook.

Bleaklow and the Upper Derwent

To the south of Longdendale is the even more daunting peat plateau of Bleaklow, rising to its highest point of 2,057ft (627m) at Bleaklow Head and crossed by the Pennine Way. Once again this is very grim-looking country, and it should be treated with great respect by walkers of all standards and levels of experience. A distinctive feature of this area is the collection of curious rock tors and crags that jut out above the moorland plateau. Many of these are marked on the Ordnance Survey map and provide very good fixing points for compass bearings.

Bleaklow Head itself is relatively easy to get at. The obvious route from the south is the Pennine Way from the Snake Road. From the north, there are several routes starting in Longdendale and leading up the steep valleys which have their headwaters in the thousands upon thousands of 'groughs' that dissect the summit plateau. A famous route from the west is along the Roman Road known as 'Doctor's Gate', picking up the Pennine Way just north of the Snake Road.

Further to the east are the wild wet moors that can offer a

Back Tor

sense of remoteness matched in England only by Dartmoor and a few other places. The similarity with Dartmoor is reinforced by the presence of the gritstone tors, particularly on the eastern ridge, where Dovestone Tor and Back Tor offer good points to aim for when starting a walk from the eastern side of the park on the outskirts of Sheffield. The bleakness is softened in the valleys – the Derwent valley itself, with its reservoirs and plantations, offers a miniature and more attractive version of Longdendale. The most attractive walking in this area, though, is neither on the ridges (insofar as they can be called ridges), nor in the main valleys, but in the smaller tributary valleys. Here, the steep slopes, the woodlands and the occasional curiosity (such as the gigantic landslip of Alport Castles) offer the variety and contrast that are the hallmarks of a good walk.

For example, if you take a bus to Alport Bridge on the Manchester–Sheffield (Snake) road, you can soon be in the beautiful valley of Alport Dale, following a track to Alport Farm. From this point there is a right of way leading eastwards and taking you up to the ridge of open country just south of Alport Castles. There is then a fine ridge walk back to the main road at the Ashopton Viaduct. This first takes you across the access land of Rowlee Pasture, and, after descending 300ft (90m), along a right of way that follows the line of a watershed between the two branches of the Ladybower reservoir.

Kinder Scout

Kinder is altogether more popular with walkers than Bleaklow or Black Hill, being nearer the mecca of Edale, but it needs to be treated with the same caution and respect. The scenery here displays many of the features found in the areas described above – notably the deep black peat and the mysterious-looking tors and crags – but the plateau summit is flatter and the surrounding slopes and valleys are much steeper. Waterfalls on the plateau edge abound, the most famous being Kinder Downfall on the western edge above the Kinder Valley itself. Many walkers start their outing at Hayfield and follow the road and tracks up to the Kinder reservoir, and then up the valley of William Clough to pick up the Pennine Way overlooking Ashophead. They then follow the Pennine Way back past Kinder Downfall and either across Kinder Low and down Jacob's Ladder, or across the centre of the plateau itself to descend to Edale via Grinds Brook.

The Dark Peak: a warning

It cannot be emphasised too strongly how exhausting walking across the peat moorlands can be once you leave defined tracks. The ground is slippery and the surface is cut up by innumerable small streams. One's sense of direction is easily distorted by the constant twists and turns that have to be made. Walking on the northern moors of the Peak District is extremely challenging and rewarding, but it carries some very special risks which should in no way be underestimated.

Mam Tor and the Hope valley

The northern gritstone moors are separated from the southern limestone plateaux and valleys by an intermediate zone of country which is full of character and beauty – and visitors! Hope, Castleton and Edale are tremendously popular centres.

For a fine view over the reservoirs and down the Derwent valley climb up to Win Hill. From there you can head north-west towards Kinder or, if you are prepared to descend some distance and then climb again, west to Lose Hill and then along the ridge between the Hope valley and Edale, past Hollins Cross and Mam Tor. This ridge walk offers splendid views, not only of the valleys on either side, but also of the black moors to the north and the 'white' limestone country to the south. Unfortunately, it is also impossible to avoid seeing the huge limestone works south of Hope.

From Mam Tor it is no great distance to the head of the Winnats, a steep, castellated, limestone valley which is one of the most famous and magnificent features of the Peak District. It's well worth a visit, even if you do have to weave your way through the traffic and the picnickers on the way down.

The western hills

The Millstone-Grit of the northern plateaux extends south-wards on either side of the southern limestone plateaux and underlies some further excellent walking country, particularly in the west.

The western moors are heavily dissected and there are few continuous ridge walks that you can make. Nevertheless, with the country falling away rapidly to the east and west, the western hills offer some very exhilarating walking within easy reach of such main towns as Macclesfield, Buxton and Leek. The countryside is also tamer and less daunting than Kinder and Bleaklow.

From Whaley Bridge in the north you can follow paths and tracks up the Goyt valley, where a famous exercise in traffic management was initiated several years ago. The upper part of the valley is periodically closed to cars, and people can gain access to picnic spots by a mini-bus. This makes walking in the valley at peak times (such as summer Sundays) much more attractive. As you walk up the valley, the scenery gradually changes from lowland to upland. A good point to aim for in a valley walk is Shining Tor, which can be reached by a track that heads south-west from the Goyt valley alongside the valley of Shooters Clough.

Shining Tor is the first of a series of summits that give views over the Cheshire Plain to the west. Three miles further south is Shutlingsloe which, although a couple of hundred feet lower than Shining Tor, stands out from the surrounding countryside in a more prominent fashion. Further to the south again is the ridge known as The Roaches and, just beyond that, the summit of Hen Cloud. These names give no clue to the utterly fantastic features to which they are attached. The Roaches is a long narrow ridge bordered on the western side by huge black cliffs and tors, while Hen Cloud is a great dark craggy peak which, but for its relatively small size, would not be out of place in the Austrian Alps.

In 1979 a serious dispute grew up over the question of public access to The Roaches, with the then owners trying to keep walkers and climbers away. After a vigorous campaign organised by the Ramblers' Association and the British Mountaineering Council, the outcome was the purchase of the land for public access by the Peak Park Planning Board.

The area of land purchased by the board includes a delightful stretch of valley woodland known as Back Forest, which contains the mysterious feature named Lud's Church. Described on the Ordnance Survey map as a cave, it is in fact a short, narrow, but very deep valley in the forest, almost hidden from sight. With its utter stillness and its overhanging crags wet with mosses and ferns, Lud's Church offers an experience on a misty early morning that no one could forget.

The Peak's western hills, therefore, offer ideal country for short, half-day walks. They contain striking and varied scenery and a number of well-defined summits which are within easy reach of main roads.

Dovedale

On the southern border of the national park is Thorpe Cloud, a steep conical limestone mound which rewards those who clamber up its 500ft (152m) slopes with a breathtaking view over the southern end of Dovedale.

From Hartington, 6 miles to the north, to Thorpe Cloud, the River Dove winds through an ever-deepening limestone valley which takes on Gothic proportions at its southern end. The overhanging trees, the rock spires and the caves provide a natural tourist attraction that is stared at and photographed by thousands of puffing visitors every year. Despite this, the path through Dovedale still offers a lovely walk, particularly between Milldale and Hartington. Here, the cliffs and rock faces give way to smooth, steep, grass slopes, the crowds thin out, and the rambler is left with one of the most enchanting riverside walks in the whole of England.

Chatsworth and the Edges

Capability Brown's Chatsworth Park is a world-famous piece of landscaping and, from the walker's point of view, offers excellent country for Sunday strolling.

To the north of Chatsworth and on the eastern slopes of the Derwent valley are the Edges – Curbar, Froggatt, Stanage and several others. The Edges mark the eastern counterpart of the western strip of gritstone hills that rise to Shining Tor and The Roaches. But this eastern range of hills is much more even, with the moors rising gently and steadily from Sheffield and the lowland country in the east to reach the long linear summit of the Edges stretching from Ladybower right down to Chatsworth. It is a really exhilarating walk to follow the tracks along the top of the Edges, there being superb views over the Derwent valley and the limestone plateaux to the west. The grunts and hammerings of rock climbers will undoubtedly accompany your journey, but they can be left to their idle and mindless pastimes as you give proper attention to the western panorama!

The valleys and plateaux of the White Peak

The southern limestone plateaux in the park are relatively bare and open, and are crossed by a network of dry-stone walls that form a distinctive but slowly disappearing feature of this country. Walkers are frequently implored, in notices put up by the park board, not to clamber over the walls and to use the stiles instead. Often these 'stiles' consist of nothing more than a thin vertical slit in the wall, leaving problems for the overweight but providing perfect sighting points when the line of the path is not otherwise clear.

The Tissington and High Peak trails offer trouble-free walking across the plateaux, but they are best used as part of a circular walk which breaks away from them at some point and takes in one or two of the delightful valleys and ravines and a couple of the attractive villages that are dotted all over the White Peak. Gratton Dale, Deep Dale, Lathkill Dale and others all offer a sharp contrast to the plateau landscape. One minute you are strolling across smooth meadows with plenty of time to indulge in cloud-watching and daydreaming and the next you are carefully picking your way down a steep rocky path that takes you into a dry limestone gorge.

The Wye valley runs from west to east across the White Peak and affords some excellent walking in its own right – particularly in its upper reaches, known successively as Chee Dale, Miller's Dale and Monsal Dale. In particular, Monsal Dale, with its wide meandering river and beautiful woodlands, offers a scene which is the quintessence of English countryside at its most beautiful. If you have only one day for walking in the Peak, make sure that Monsal Dale falls along the route that you choose.

To sample some of these contrasts in scenery, try the following walk from Bakewell to Tideswell. From the centre of Bakewell, follow streets and paths south-eastwards through the town between the A6 and the River Wye. Just before reaching Haddon House, cross the A6 and follow the trackway that eventually leads up to the village of Over Haddon. There is then a steep drop into the beautiful wooded ravine of Lathkill Dale, which can be followed upstream along the northern bank through a nature reserve. The path eventually comes out on to the limestone plateau again near the village of Monyash.

From here, take fieldpaths northwards across to the top of Deep Dale. Follow the path which runs along the bottom of this rocky, wooded, dry valley and suddenly emerges into the

Monsal Dale and Longstone Edge, from Fin Cop

magnificent country of the Upper Wye valley. A path now takes you through Monsal Dale, along the western side of the valley at the foot of long, wooded slopes. The dale curves round smoothly and brings you out by the famous railway viaduct below Monsal Head. It is now possible to follow this disused railway line on foot, but for the purpose of this walk, keep to the low ground and cross the river to follow a country lane on its northern side to Cressbrook. After this point there is a path going through the winding ravine of Miller's Dale, past a small factory, and then up into Tideswell Dale and so on up to Tideswell itself. Limestone crags appear everywhere on the final sections of this walk and make this an extremely enchanting piece of country.

5
The Yorkshire Dales

The Dales National Park is perhaps best known for its spectacular limestone scenery – the finest in Britain. Malham Cove, Gordale Scar, Gaping Gill Hole – these names are familiar to tourists and O-level students alike, and they evoke visions of awe-inspiring landforms that never fail to amaze. They are all accessible on foot and, as is so often the case in the national parks, the true splendour of these landscapes can be fully appreciated only by the walker.

The dales from which the national park takes its name are also, of course, to be counted among the chief attractions of this area. Each dale is distinct in character and comparisons are invidious, but one is inclined to agree with that much respected author of walkers' books on Northern England, Wainwright, when he classes Swaledale and Wharfedale as being the best of all. These broad valleys, with their strong-flowing rivers, their steep wooded slopes, their ancient Norse villages, and their beautiful combination of green meadows, stone walls and grass- or heather-clad upper slopes and ridges, offer walking country of a rare quality. It is hardly surprising that one of the most popular of the country's 'unofficial' long-distance paths is the Dales Way, which follows field and riverside paths from Ilkley along the length of Wharfedale and its upper section, Langstrothdale, to Dentdale and thence to the Lake District. It is described in Colin Speakman's Dalesman book.

Equally popular, but utterly different in character, is a 26-mile route known as the Three Peaks Walk. This exacting trek links the three outstanding peaks of Pen-y-Ghent, Whernside and Ingleborough in a circular route. But, first-class hill walk as it is, it is really not one that gives a typical picture of fell walking in the Dales National Park; if anything, its character is more in keeping with that of the Lake District. For the fells of

51

Smearsett Scar, near Settle, from Pot Scar

the Yorkshire Dales are very much of the Pennines – gentle
swells surrounded by what seem to be vast areas of upland
wilderness. For the most part, the open moors of the national
park are lonely, peat-covered expanses that are worlds apart
from the industrial areas of Teesside and West Yorkshire, from
whence most of the passionate hill-walking enthusiasts of the
Dales National Park come. The total change of environment
is, of course, very much part of the attraction.

One of the most memorable stretches of Britain's number-
one long-distance path, the Pennine Way, passes through the

national park. The Way runs for 54 miles through the Yorkshire Dales, entering the park in the south near Gargrave and
leaving it in the north at the high and lonely staging post of
Tan Hill. The path offers a superb south–north traverse of the
park, and one that can be broken down into manageable stages
between centres such as Malham, Horton in Ribblesdale,
Hawes and Keld.

After passing through woods and pastures in the Aire valley
above Gargrave, the Pennine Way suddenly comes upon the
natural amphitheatre of Malham Cove. Beyond this, the
scenery changes dramatically. First, there is the traverse of
bare limestone pavement; then the skirting of Malham Tarn;
and after this, the steady climb across open moors to the

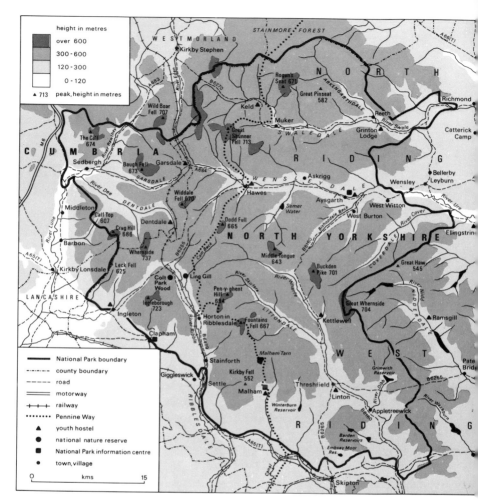

summit of Fountains Fell, from which the first high-level view
of the Yorkshire Dales and their peaks is obtained. After Fountains Fell comes the scramble up Pen-y-Ghent and the easy
descent to Horton, passing close by the fearsome limestone
caverns known as Hunt Pot and Hull Pot.

The stretch from Horton to Hawes can convey a feeling of
utter remoteness, and this is reinforced by the historical associ-
ations of some of the tracks followed en route. First there is an
old packhorse road running from Horton to Birkwith Moor
between gleaming white limestone walls and then later, a
stretch of the Roman Road that connected Ingleton with the

54

Roman fort at Bainbridge. (These old green lanes soon become a familiar and welcome feature to the walker in the Yorkshire Dales and are a delight to follow. Mastiles Lane, which connects Wharfedale and Malhamdale, is another such trackway. It was used by medieval monasteries and later for the transport of lead. Today these ancient routes are used mainly by walkers and farmers, although motorcyclists are claiming a right of passage and are using them more and more. This is a practice which surely needs to be curbed.)

The descent to Hawes along the Pennine Way offers one of the best vistas of Wensleydale. Similarly, the descent along the Way into Swaledale further north affords magnificent views down that valley as well. Between the two dales lies Great Shunner Fell, which is crossed by the Way and from where, on a clear day, the unmistakable peaks of the Lake District mountains can be seen.

The Hawes–Keld section of the Pennine Way is an excellent walk in its own right. First, it passes close by Hardrow Force – a 90ft (27m) waterfall that you can actually scramble round the back of if you have the nerve. Then there is the long, steady climb to Great Shunner Fell, with views opening out all round as more and more height is gained. Next, there is the descent to Swaledale at Thwaite, and finally, the pièce de résistance, the loop from Thwaite to Keld along a limestone terrace overlooking the perfectly formed and traffic-free valley cut by the River Swale. As Keld is approached, there are the famous waterfalls – Kisdon Force, with its two falls set in a steep, wooded, limestone gorge; East Gill Force, where a tributary joins from the north; and Catrake Force, lying right below Keld itself.

The waterfalls lie on the route of another long-distance path – the Coast to Coast Walk. This enters the national park high above the 2,000ft (610m) contour near Nine Standards Rigg (a summit just outside the park boundary), and then descends into Swaledale to the Keld waterfalls through little-known moorland country (little known, that is, until Wainwright invented what is now one of the most popular of long-distance walks). It then takes an unusual route north of the dale, across high country that is notable for its extensive remains of buildings and workings connected with the former lead mining industry of this area. This makes it a most fascinating walk for

people with a special interest in industrial archaeology.

Apart from the long-distance paths, there are many shorter trails and well-trodden walks in the park. The Three Peaks Walk has already been mentioned. This is described in *The Big Walks* and can be picked out clearly from Arthur Gemmell's Three Peaks footpath map – one of a series referred to in more detail in the Appendix.

At the other end of the walking spectrum are the easy but still very delightful nature trails in the woods close to Bolton Abbey, in the south-eastern corner of the park. There are several miles of walks in these woods, through which runs the River Wharfe. At one point known as the Strid, the river runs, seething and boiling, through a narrow chasm – a sight to be seen, but not a place for crossing the river! There is, incidentally, a small fee for entering these woods. Some people think that it's an imposition which offers a precedent for setting up tolls for walkers through the countryside; others, more generously disposed, think it's fair that the public should be asked to contribute to the upkeep of these beautiful woods.

Another special trail is the 4-mile Reginald Farrer Trail, which starts at the national park centre in Clapham and follows the valley of Clapham Beck past the show caverns of Ingleborough Cave to the wooded ravine of Trow Gill. This is an easy and fascinating walk, and one which provides a good introduction to the limestone scenery of the Yorkshire Dales. There is an impressive number of other waymarked walks, for the most part less than 8 miles in length. They begin at such centres as Dent, Aysgarth, Stainforth, Clapham, Kettlewell, Hawes and Reeth.

The national park office also runs a full programme of guided walks from April to October. They are led by guides with specialist local knowledge, starting from national park centres and lasting for most of the afternoon. A charge is made and advance booking is often necessary; a programme is available from the national park office.

For the walker who prefers to make his or her own way, there are over 1,000 miles of public footpaths and bridleways

(opposite) The village of Thwaite in Swaledale

in the park, all marked on OS maps. Public access has also been secured by agreement with the landowner to 14,000 acres of hill land on Barden Fell and Barden Moor, south of Grassington. These fells – used for grouse shooting – were the subject of much controversy prior to access agreements being signed, with walkers frequently being 'seen off' by eagle-eyed gamekeepers. There is also, of course, de facto access to most of the open moorland country in the park. However, reports do reach the RA from time to time of people being turned back when they are on open country but not on a right of way. Our right to roam across the hills will not be fully secured until legislation is passed granting access on foot to all open country – something that the RA has been fighting for for years.

Another thing that the RA has been working for in the Yorkshire Dales is better public transport. Here, there have been some striking successes, much to the benefit of the walker. After a pioneering effort by the RA (inspired by Colin Speakman, the man who deserves all the credit for this scheme), the national park committee set up the service now known as Dalesrail. On eight weekends in the year, from April to October, this provides a rail service from Leeds and other population centres to the formerly closed stations along the Settle–Carlisle line, such as Garsdale and Horton. There are connecting buses at Garsdale and guided walks are organised in connection with this service. Local people make use of the return trips by travelling to the West Riding to shop and visit friends. Leaflets giving full details of this service, and of the connecting links and guided walks, are available from national park centres or from Dalesrail, Metro House, West Parade, Wakefield WF1 1NS.

Another public transport service, set up more recently, is the 'Parklink' scheme. This is based on Wharfedale and, under the scheme, the walker can buy a reduced-price ticket from a main station in West Yorkshire and use it to take the train to Skipton and then a bus into Wharfedale, as far as Buckden if desired. Arthur Gemmell has produced a booklet, *Parklink Walks*, in which a number of fine walks in Upper Wharfedale are described with the Parklink user in mind.

Other public transport services in the park have been subject to the familiar cuts of recent years, but bus services still run in many dales, and full information is available in a 'Transport Information Pack' available from the national park office in Grassington. Literature produced by the national park office emphasises the need for walkers to go well prepared if they are venturing on to the hills. The Pennines can be very inhospitable, even in summer. There are also the special dangers of limestone country – the potholes and the caves, the clints and the grykes. The weird landforms of this area deserve careful inspection; but don't get too close to the edge of a sheer drop. Finally, the walker should always be on the alert when crossing country that has been subject in the past to mining. For example, the lead mining area of Swaledale and the coal mining airshafts near Tan Hill are places to be wary of.

Grassington and Malhamdale

Although lacking in height compared to other parts of the park, the south-eastern corner contains some spectacular limestone scenery and offers very good riverside and hill-walking country. From Bolton Abbey to Grassington, for example, the Dales Way long-distance path runs hard by the River Wharfe, passing through beautiful woodlands and by the delightful stone-built village of Burnsall. From the valley, the walker can break off and climb up on to the open country of Barden Moor to the west, or (and perhaps rather more interesting and rewarding) Barden Fell to the east. Around Grassington there is a dense network of paths (all shown clearly on one of Mr Gemmell's maps). These can be combined to make short walks taking in the fields, valleys and curious limestone knolls around the villages of Threshfield, Linton and Thorpe; or they can be followed on to the open heather moors above Grassington. (But beware – there are some old mineshafts in this part.)

A varied and fascinating walk in this area can be had by starting at Grassington (well served by public transport) and following the Dales Way upriver along the eastern bank of the Wharfe, through Grass Wood to Conistone. From here, cross the river to Kilnsey, close to which is the bulky, overhanging, limestone cliff known as Kilnsey Crag. Then climb up on to

the limestone plateau, following Mastiles Lane. There are fine views back across Wharfedale. Shortly after crossing Gordale Beck, follow a path that leads south-east to Gordale Scar – a huge ravine formed by the collapse of a roof over an underground cavern. After scrambling down the scar itself, follow the beck down to the pretty waterfall of Janets Foss. The path eventually joins the Pennine Way, which can be followed back to Malham. From here, there is an optional out-and-back walk to admire the cove. The whole of this walk can be followed using Gemmell's maps for the Grassington and Malhamdale areas.

Upper Wharfedale, Littondale and Langstrothdale

The country around Upper Wharfedale takes on a mature and lofty aspect. The hills rise steeply to the imposing summits of Great Whernside, Buckden Pike and Fountains Fell, and the dales are wide, wooded and lush.

Once again, the Dales Way provides an excellent walk through the dales of this part of the national park. From above Conistone to Kettlewell, it follows a limestone terrace running parallel to the valley and overlooking it. It then descends to the floor of the valley to follow the river past Buckden and into Langstrothdale. This is a particularly pleasant part of the Way, because the path runs alongside the river, which flows over bare, smooth limestone and is bordered by unfenced grassy banks. It is an idyllic setting. Higher up, the Way follows Oughtershaw Beck and climbs on to higher ground, thereby just avoiding a most outrageous and unpleasant conifer plantation in Upper Langstrothdale, the introduction of which caused an outcry in 1970. This is what much of the Pennines would look like if the government acceded to pressure from the forestry lobby for a massive expansion of the afforested area in upland Britain.

The long broad valley of Littondale is also well served by paths and tracks, and many walks along it or across its limestone-terraced slopes are possible. The OS 2½in Outdoor

(*opposite*) Gordale Scar

Leisure Map of Malham and Upper Wharfedale is an excellent guide to the paths in this area, as it is to the whole of the south-central part of the national park.

Some of the tributary streams that run into the Wharfe and the Skirfare (Littondale) run through very dramatic valleys that can be visited by following paths in this area. For example, the path that climbs out of Arncliffe heading across the limestone moors to Malham overlooks the narrow, steep-sided valley of Cowside Beck. Paths running eastwards from Kettlewell take you through or close to the quite stunning valleys of Park Gill Beck and Dowber Gill Beck. A number of them lead on to the open hill slopes that rise to the summit of Great Whernside. The routes are described in one or two of the guide-books mentioned in the Appendix and can easily be followed from the Outdoor Leisure Map. Great Whernside overlooks Upper Nidderdale to the east. There is some excellent walking country here as well, but for some reason this dale was left out of the national park.

To the north-west of Whernside is another imposing summit – Buckden Pike. The favoured ascent of this peak is from Buckden. A track leads northwards through Rakes Wood before turning across open country to the summit. The first part of this walk is especially attractive, there being wide views across the valley to the beautiful wooded slopes opposite. To the north you overlook the large waterfall near Cray.

Fountains Fell, the other main summit in this area, is more remote. A full day's walk that takes in Fountains Fell – rather hard but well worth the effort – is as follows. Start at Buckden and follow the Dales Way through Langstrothdale (whose praises were sung earlier on) to Yockenthwaite. From here, take the path that climbs south-westwards to the watershed at Horse Head Gate. Descend to Halton Gill in Littondale and walk alongside the unfenced road signposted for Stainforth. This route gives superb views down Littondale and over the steep tributary valley followed by Pen-y-Ghent Gill. The road is eventually intersected by the Pennine Way, which takes you directly up to the summit of Fountains Fell. At this point, either follow the Pennine Way back to Malham or turn north across open country to pick up the trackway that leads down to Litton. Gather your strength and then follow the path that leads on to the flat-topped ridge of Old Cote Moor and from there directly down to Buckden. This walk – which takes in much of the heart of the Yorkshire Dales – is well worth getting into shape for. It can be followed by using the Outdoor Leisure Map.

The Three Peaks area

This is perhaps the most renowned sector of the national park, containing the nationally-famous Three Peaks Walk that has already been referred to. With the Outdoor Leisure Map, Mr Gemmel's Three Peaks footpath map and a number of guides and leaflets describing walks in this area, the walker is well served.

Of the three summits, Whernside is the highest (indeed, the highest in the national park) but, not enjoying quite the same

Pen-y-Ghent, from Rainscar, near Horton in Ribblesdale

degree of splendid isolation as the other two, it is also the least popular. The nearest point from which to strike out for Whernside is Ribblehead, but for those who prefer a longer walk with plenty of time to relish the steady gain of height, there is a route from Ingleton village. This follows country lanes to Scar End and then, after a sharp climb over Twistelton Scar End, there is a very long, dead-straight trek along the ridge to the summit.

Pen-y-Ghent is the most mountainous-looking of the three summits and is no great distance from Horton. Nevertheless, it gives you a real sense of achievement to attain the highest point, no matter how short the journey. The real giant of the three, however, is Ingleborough. Its wide, flat-topped summit (on which there actually was a prehistoric fort) is flanked by steep slopes and crags on all sides, giving Ingleborough a Massada-like appearance. On the surrounding limestone plateau are Gaping Gill Hole, passed on the popular route to the top from Clapham, and limestone pavements on a grand scale. The climb from Ingleton is also well defined, and a complete traverse, starting at Ingleton and then descending from the summit to Horton along the route followed by Three Peaks Walk, is one of the best hill traverses of a single summit in the Pennines.

There is also plenty to admire lower down in this area. The Reginald Farrer Nature Trail starting at Clapham has already been mentioned. There is, too, the 4½-mile tour of the waterfalls on the rivers above Ingleton. The paths and bridges on this walk (for which you may be charged a fee at some point) were laid out in Victorian times. The walk follows the River Doe to Beezley Falls, then crosses to the Kingsdale Beck at Thornton Force and so back to Ingleton past more falls, woods and cliffs. It is a charming short walk, just right for a summer evening after a day on the hills.

The western dales and fells

The national park boundary extends westwards to embrace two of the quieter dales — Dentdale and Garsdale — and the southern section of those unique rolling hills known as the Howgills.

The Dales Way, having crossed the Pennine watershed after leaving Wharfedale, runs down through Dentdale and once again offers a prime walking route through the valley. Dentdale has an ancient air about it; not yet overrun by tourists, it retains all the colour and intimate variety in its scenery that are lost in areas where modern buildings have been allowed to dominate. Garsdale is also remote, but it has a busier road running through it.

Where Dentdale and Garsdale meet, near Sedbergh, there are some delightful riverside walks, one or two of which are described in national park leaflets. The 'Rawthey Way' is the name given to the riverside path south of Sedbergh, and although it can be followed only for a mile or two in either direction, it is ideal for pleasant summer evening strolls.

Looming over Sedbergh are the Howgills – smooth, steep and rounded open fells that are totally different in nature from the rest of the national park. Here, there are no limestone pavements and disappearing rivers, or expanses of peat-bog. Instead, there are steep slopes and deep winding valleys everywhere. Unfortunately, only the southern part of the Howgills are in the national park, but this does include the highest point, The Calf, and the giant precipice known as Cautley Crag.

Sedbergh is an excellent centre from which to explore the Howgills. A walk which lies within the national park – and which can be followed on yet another of Arthur Gemmell's maps – starts at Sedbergh and follows paths and tracks alongside and later parallel with the River Rawthey to the Cautley Holme Beck. The valley of this stream is then followed on to the open fell, with Cautley Crag being avoided by passing to the north. You can then quickly gain the highest point, The Calf, and from here, smooth, windy ridges take you back to the summit of Winder, which directly overlooks Sedbergh and from which a quick descent can be made.

Part of the route described above is incorporated in the 23-mile trek from Kirkby Stephen to Sedbergh described in *The Big Walks*. This walk takes in Wild Boar Fell which, although outside the park boundary, is, as Colin Speakman describes it, 'one of the most magnificent mountains in the north of England'. It is certainly prominent in all the views from summits in the north-western part of the park, and the climb to the summit, with its steep east-facing crags, is breathtaking in more senses than one. In his book *Walking in the Craven Dales*, Colin Speakman describes a 14-mile circular walk that starts at Garsdale Head, takes in Wild Boar Fell, and then returns on the other side of the Eden valley along a prehistoric trackway known as the High Way. It must rank as one of the most exciting and interesting walks in the Yorkshire Dales, and the fact that half of it lies outside the national park testifies to the need for a review of the park boundary in this area.

Wensleydale

Wensleydale is the longest of the Yorkshire dales and runs across the whole width of the northern part of the national park. Its broad, rolling, moraine-filled valley is flanked on both sides by limestone terraces and moorland ridges, with the southern slopes being dissected by long valleys such as Coverdale and Bishopdale. The scope for valley-and-ridge walks is therefore enormous.

At its eastern end are Aysgarth Falls – the first place that any newcomer to the area should visit. There are in fact three main waterfalls. They are set in a beautiful wooded gorge, and can be seen on a short but excellent walk starting at the national park centre north of Yore Bridge. From here, the walks to the falls are very popular and clearly defined. For a longer stroll of nearly 7 miles, follow fieldpaths across to Castle Bolton and return via Carperby. A national park leaflet available from the centre describes the route, which can also be followed from the OS map.

Facing Castle Bolton, on the south side of the valley, is the towering plateau of Penhill. This is also worth a visit, and it can be reached in a short walk from the minor road running from West Witton to Melmerby. A bridleway leads from the road to the summit. The views eastwards across the Vale of York to the North York Moors are superb.

The footpaths, bridleways and green lanes that run across the slopes bordering Wensleydale offer scope for many fine walks. Particularly to be recommended is the fieldpath route from Bainbridge to Semerwater. The lake can be sublimely

Aysgarth Lower Falls in Wensleydale

beautiful on a clear, quiet day. You can extend the valley walk to Marsett, then turn north-west to reach the Roman Road and return along the ridge to Bainbridge, with views across Wensleydale on the way.

On the northern slopes, there is a lovely short walk from Askrigg. This starts near the church and follows rights of way alongside Mill Gill, passing close by a number of waterfalls, to Askey Top, a lane that leads back to the village while affording extensive views across the main valley below.

Swaledale

Swaledale is perhaps the most strikingly beautiful of all the dales. The best afternoon's circular walk in this valley (and it is perhaps the best in the national park) is from Keld to Muker and back again. There are various ways in which this can be done, but a route to be recommended starts at Park Bridge, which is a little way above Keld and close by the highest of Keld's waterfalls, Wain Wath Force. Follow the track to the north of the river, with views over the falls below. The route comes down to the Swale again by East Gill Force and then climbs steeply up the southern bank along the route of the Pennine Way. Drop down to visit Kisdon Force – the most picturesque of them all – and then climb back to rejoin the footpath that leads along the valley floor to Muker. This village, like Keld, is beautifully preserved and appears to be almost untouched by the twentieth century. By way of a return route, follow the bridleway over Kisdon Hill for a bird's-eye view of Swaledale.

Further downstream, Arkengarthdale, a northern tributary of Swaledale, repays careful exploration – it is a little-frequented corner of the national park, but extremely attractive nevertheless. Walks starting and finishing at Reeth, a stately looking market town, can be planned to take in views of both Arkengarthdale and this part of Swaledale. For example, follow the lane along the Swale valley to Marrick Priory, then climb to Marrick and follow the top of Fremington Edge before descending again to Reeth. Alternatively, follow paths along the north-eastern bank of the Arkle Beck upstream from Reeth as far as Arkle Town. Then cross the river and take one of the paths leading on to Cringley Hill, with views over to the steep, wooded slopes of Arkengarthdale above Langthwaite. Pass to the west of Calver Hill and descend to Reeth along that hill's southern slopes. The latter part of this route follows the Coast to Coast Walk along a stretch that Wainwright commends for its views.

6

The North York Moors

The distinct and isolated block of hills known as the North York Moors will be familiar to most walkers through their association with that most popular of all long-distance walks, the Lyke Wake Walk. Today, the 40-mile trek across the spine of the moors, from Osmotherley in the west to the coast at Ravenscar, is marked by a wide track through the heather that has been created by the thousands of walkers that attempt the crossing every year.

It's a good walk; but it serves its purpose best if it convinces the walker who is new to the moors that there is far more to the national park than can be appreciated in a blind charge from one end to the other. The first 10 miles of the walk, across the Cleveland Hills, is but one section (albeit the most majestic) of the long escarpment that marks the western and northern boundaries of the park. The long stretch across the central moors can, in the right weather conditions, afford magnificent skyscapes and sweeping views that give a sense of spaciousness unmatched by any other scenery in England. Within closer range are long, broad valleys – such as Rosedale and Farndale to the south and Eskdale to the north – that offer riverside and woodland walks of national renown. And finally, there is the coastline, where the moors meet the sea along towering cliffs that afford exhilarating and strenuous walking along the Cleveland Way long-distance path.

All this is contained within a national park that at no point rises above 1,500ft (457m). But what the national park lacks in height, it makes up for in the stately shape of its landforms and in the colour and expanse of its central feature – the heather moorlands. The moors, however, are by no means as extensive as they once were. In fact, in recent years the rate at which the open moors have been converted to forestry or enclosed pasture has been quite alarming. One estimate has it that

70

44,000 acres of moorland were lost during the period 1950–1980. That is about 25 per cent of the moorland area. In some areas, the loss has not been serious – indeed, the addition of small areas of enclosed green pasture-land on the edge of the moorland plateau can sometimes add variety to the scene. But where the moorland has been converted wholesale to conifer plantations (as it has in much of the south-eastern part of the national park) or cultivated land, the loss to walkers is very serious. One has only to look at Exmoor to see what could happen to the North York Moors if moorland conversion is not brought under control soon.

The moors have received great attention from the writers of walks guides and the planners of long-distance paths. The Lyke Wake Walk – already referred to – is described in Bill Cowley's Dalesman book and summarised in a chapter in *The Big Walks*. The national park office produces a very useful set of notes for those planning to accomplish this walk. It gives advice on clothing, safety, organisation of support parties, transport and access. It is striking that much of the route does not follow rights of way, de facto access across the moors having never been seriously challenged. However, if you are planning to do the walk, please seek up-to-date information from the national park office, because the starting and finishing points have recently been changed slightly to avoid problems in the villages at either end.

The 'official' long-distance path for the North York Moors is, of course, the Cleveland Way. This follows a 100-mile horseshoe-shaped route from Helmsley, along the Hambleton and Cleveland hills to Guisborough and the coast, and then back along the cliffs past Whitby and Scarborough to Filey. The HMSO guide to the Cleveland Way is a first-class publication and it contains some particularly good photographs and also 1:25,000 maps for the whole route. Malcolm Boyes' guide, published by Constable, also describes a link from Scarborough to Helmsley for those wishing to make a circular trip.

Another west–east crossing of the moor – and actually a rather better one than the Lyke Wake Walk – is described by Wainwright in *A Coast to Coast Walk*. In essence, it follows the line of the Cleveland Way and Lyke Wake Walk from

71

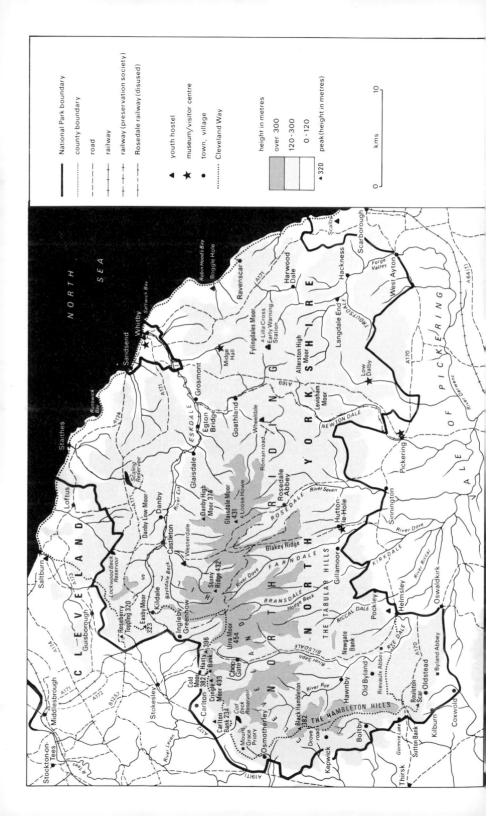

National Park boundary
county boundary
road
railway
railway (preservation society)
Rosedale railway (disused)

▲ youth hostel
★ museum/visitor centre
● town, village
⋯⋯ Cleveland Way

height in metres
over 300
120-300
0-120
▲ 320 peak (height in metres)

kms
0   10

NORTH   SEA

Staithes
Loftus
Saltburn
Guisborough
Middlesbrough
Stockton-on-Tees

Sandsend
Whitby
Saltwick Bay
Runswick Bay

Robin Hood's Bay
Boggle Hole
Ravenscar

CLEVELAND

Scaling Reservoir
Lockwood Beck Reservoir
Roseberry Topping 320
Easby Moor 323
Kildale
Ingleby Greenhow
Cold Moor 392
Carlton Moor 392
Carlton Bank 234
Cringle Moor 433
Hasty Bank 396
Chop Gate
Urra Moor 454
Mount Grace Priory
Osmotherley
Cod Beck Reservoir
Black Hambleton 382
Drove road

Danby Low Moor
Danby
Castleton
Westerdale
Bransdale Beck
Danby High Moor 374
Glaisdale Moor
Stony Ridge 432
Blakey Ridge
Loose Howe

ESKDALE
River Esk
Glaisdale
Egton Bridge
Grosmont
Goathland
Wheeldale
Roman road

Fylingdales Moor
▲ Lilla Cross
Early Warning Station
Midge Hall
Harwood Dale
Allerston High Moor

RIDING

YORKSHIRE

NEWTON DALE
Langdale End
Low Dalby

Levisham Moor

Scarborough
▲ Scalby
Hackness
Forge Valley
West Ayton

VALE   OF   PICKERING

A171
A169
A170
A64(T)
River Derwent

Rosedale Abbey
ROSEDALE
River Seven
Hutton-le-Hole

FARNDALE
River Dove
BRANSDALE
Hodge Beck

NORTH

THE TABULAR HILLS

KIRKDALE
River Dove
Sinnington
Pickering

RICCAL DALE
Gillamoor
Pockley
Helmsley
Oswaldkirk
River Riccal

BILSDALE
River Seph
RYE DALE
Newgate Bank
Rievaulx Abbey
Hawnby
Old Byland
Byland Abbey
Oldstead

MOORLAND

YORK

THE HAMBLETON HILLS
Boltby
Kepwick
Roulston Scar
Sutton Bank
Thirsk
Kilburn
Coxwold
Gormire Lake

Stokesley
Stokton-on-Tees

A172
A173
A174
A171
A174
A172
B1257
A170
A19(T)
River Leven
River Tees
River Rye

Osmotherley to Rosedale, but then heads north-east into Eskdale to sample the delights of woods and waterfalls in that area. It then passes through Hawsker to finish, with a sweep along the coastline, at Robin Hood's Bay.

Other long-distance creations include the White Rose Walk, described in a book by Geoffrey White. This links the White Horse of Kilburn in the south with Roseberry Topping – Cleveland's Matterhorn – in the north. Although the walk follows the Cleveland Way for much of its route, variations are possible in the central section. Inspired by the success of the Lyke Wake Walk, the White Rose Walk bases part of its appeal on the fact that successful walkers can buy a white rose badge to wear on their rucksacks. Collectors of badges will also want to go on the Bilsdale Circuit, a 30-mile walk referred to in the section below on the Cleveland Hills. Finally, the Derwent Way (created by Richard Kenchington) is to be recommended to North York Moors walkers, because although only part of its route falls within the national park, it offers perhaps the best walk in the south-eastern section of the park (see Newton-dale and the Derwent valley below).

There is a good deal of literature describing shorter walks in the park. Much of this has been produced by the national park office and reflects the diligence and imagination of the people who work there. There are short walks from easily accessible starting points such as Grosmont, Pickering, and Rosedale Abbey, as well as from the national park centre at Danby Lodge in Eskdale. Special trails include the May Beck Trail, 5 miles south of Whitby, which is designed to show the visitor and the student some aspects of land use and management in the park; the Ravenscar Geological Trail; the Sutton Bank Trail, which is of great interest to naturalists; and the Historical Railway Trail, which runs from Goathland to Grosmont through beautiful valley country close by the railway line.

There are also a number of trails laid out by the Forestry Commission in its extensive plantations in the national park. Many walkers will find the new forests to be dull and lacking in interest, but there is no doubt that the commission has gone to a lot of trouble to open its forests to members of the public and to provide facilities for them. It produces a map of its forests in the national park and this highlights the trails that have been laid out near the White Horse of Kilburn; in the huge Dalby and Wykeham forests in the south-east; and by the Falling Foss waterfall south of Whitby. The Falling Foss walk is a particularly attractive and popular one, and the commission has produced a special leaflet to describe it. Leaflets are also available for a number of other forest trails. These include the Silpho Forest Walk along the escarpment overlooking Harwood Dale; the Sneverdale Forest Trail starting from Low Dalby; forest walks from Newtondale Halt on the Pickering–Grosmont line; and the 16-mile Reasty to Allerston Forest Walk through the Langdale and Dalby forests.

For those who prefer the open spaces, however, one of the most enchanting short walks in the national park is the Bridestones Moor Nature Walk, which is east of the Pickering–Whitby road on the northern edge of Dalby Forest. This walk runs through an area almost entirely surrounded by plantations, but preserved as open country by the National Trust. It passes by the curious-looking Low and High Bridestones – rocks that stand out like huge petrified mushrooms overlooking the valley below. A leaflet describing the walk is available from information centres in the park.

Despite the abundance of literature on the bookshelves, the best guide for the walker is still the 1in Ordnance Survey Tourist Map of the North York Moors. This shows the open country – to which there is, and has been for centuries, a de facto right of access without restriction as far as one can tell. The map also depicts rights of way, of which there are over 1,100 miles in the national park. Most of them are in a walkable condition.

Access to the moors is now becoming doubly assured through the intervention of the Treasury (of all people). The North York Moors Annual Report for 1979/80 tells how the owners of the moorland estate surrounding Bransdale have been given exemption from capital transfer tax 'in return for a guarantee that the estate's present character will be retained and extensive public access granted'. With much of the moorland in the national park being held as part of large estates, it is possible that similar safeguards will be secured for other areas over the next few years.

The national park is richly endowed with historical remains

of all kinds. As on Dartmoor, many of these features can be properly appreciated only by the walker. This is because the only means of reaching many of the remains – such as the prehistoric Bronze Age cairns and burial mounds, the medieval crosses and the disused railway lines – is on foot. One of the most striking monuments is the exposed Roman Road across Wheeldale Moor. Here, the 15ft carriageway, made of flat stones laid over a gravel base and properly drained with culverts and gulleys, is followed by a public right of way – demonstrably one of the oldest in the country! Away over to the west, across the crest of the Hambleton Hills, is the famous drove road that formed part of a route along which cattle were taken from Scotland to the south. Today, the northern part of this drove road is followed by the Cleveland Way and is one of the most notable high level green lanes in the country. Measures should be taken soon to prohibit vehicular traffic along the track, otherwise it will quickly become a gathering ground for trail riders and scramblers alike.

An historic track of very different origins is to be found winding its way around the head of Rosedale along the 1,300ft (396m) contour. This is the track of the former Rosedale Ironstone Railway, which was constructed in the middle of the last century to take iron ore from Rosedale across the moors to Teesdale. The line was closed in 1929, but the track offers a splendid walking route across the heart of the moors. It has been put to good use by the devisers of the Lyke Wake Walk and the Coast to Coast Walk, and is one of the most exciting disused railway line walks in the country.

Public transport to and within the national park is rather patchy, but good in parts. There are good bus and rail services to Scarborough and Whitby. Bus services generally are operated by United Automobile Services Ltd (United House, Grange Road, Darlington DL1 5NL). Special Wanderbus tickets, allowing unlimited travel for one day, are available during the summer months. Cleveland Transit (Parliament Road, Middlesbrough, Cleveland) also operate services in the north-western part of the park.

The Esk valley railway line to Whitby is one of the most picturesque in the country, and the stations along the line – Danby, Lealholm, Egton Bridge and other such delightful-sounding places – are excellent starting points for walks that can quickly take you into high country. Perhaps even more striking is the Grosmont–Pickering line, now run as a private line with strong backing from the national park committee. The development of this line as a tourist attraction is one of the most imaginative projects ever to have been undertaken in a national park. From the walker's point of view, the line (along which there is approximately hourly service in the peak period) gives access to superb country that cannot be reached by car or bus. The dramatic valley of Newtondale, which was formed by glacial melt-waters during the Ice Age and through which the railway runs, is itself a natural walking route. And only a short, albeit rather steep, walk away are the high moors and forests of the eastern section of the national park. Leaflets available from information centres and the main stations give details about waymarked walks along the route, and the national park office is building up a guided-walks programme based at stops along the line. The park office also organises guided walks from such centres as Sutton Bank and Danby Lodge; these are very popular and the programme of walks will no doubt be expanded in future years.

The fact that all land in the national park lies below 1,500ft (457m) should not lull the walker into a false sense of security about the potential dangers of the area. North-east winds rushing in from the coast can cause the sudden arrival of the most daunting snowstorms and blizzards – even in late spring. The expanse of the moors means that route-finding in misty conditions can be tricky, and careful compass work is called for. Walkers on the Lyke Wake Walk are advised to take special care. A 24-hour weather service is available by phoning 0632 326453.

Clifftop walking carries its obvious dangers. The Cleveland Way is susceptible to erosion at a number of points. Where you see a warning sign advising an alternative route, don't fail to heed it. Another danger in the park is that of finding unexploded shells on the moors. This is a particular risk on Fylingdales Moor, which was used as a service training area for many years. If you see a suspicious metal object leave it alone, but take a careful note of its location and inform the police as soon as possible.

One final danger to be aware of is fire. The moors were devastated by fires during the 1976 drought and the unsightly effects will be there for all to see for many years. The North York Moors don't receive nearly as much rainfall as the Lake District or even the Yorkshire Dales, and they dry out very quickly. The simple rule to adopt is don't smoke while on the moors and don't light any fires. And if you do see flames, or even just smouldering, tell someone in authority fast.

The Hambleton Hills and Ryedale

The westernmost hills of the national park offer one of the finest escarpment walks in the country. From the White Horse of Kilburn to the Sneck Yate Bank above Boltby, the Cleveland Way follows the edge of what is, in parts, literally a sheer cliff overlooking the Vale of York and the Pennines beyond.

The view from the track along the scarp across the beautiful Lake Gormire is breathtaking, and the paths around the lake itself afford some delectable short walks. North of Sneck Yate Bank, the walk along the drove road over Black Hambleton is set back from the edge of the high ground, but is nevertheless a superb moorland ridge walk. Between Ryedale and the scarp is the cultivated plateau of land marked on the OS map as the Hambleton Hills. Here there are echoes of the White Peak, because cut deeply into the limestone plateau are narrow, sinuous, wooded valleys that carry the shallow tributaries into the Rye. The sudden plunge from the open, windy plateau to the lushness and calm of one of these valleys is the sort of experience that makes one addicted to rambling – it is unique to walking. And adding to the natural glories of this area are the majestic remains of Rievaulx Abbey, set in the beautiful surroundings of Ryedale itself.

A good starting point for walks in this area is the Sutton Bank Information Centre. For a round walk of 12 miles or so across the Hambleton Hills and into Ryedale, begin by following the Cleveland Way eastwards – first along the main road back to the Hambleton Hotel and then along tracks across the plateau to Cold Kirby. One mile east of this village, the path suddenly plunges into a little wooded ravine and then runs through a most delightful tributary valley of the Rye to the fine old stone bridge just past Ashbery Farm. Now walk up to Rievaulx and the abbey itself, and after this, follow tracks and paths up the valley to Barnclose Farm.

Climb back up on to the plateau and follow the path that runs along the edge of the forest overlooking Ryedale. On reaching the metalled lane near Murton Grange, you will find there is a superb view northwards across wide deep valleys to the high moors beyond. There is then an uneventful mile or two's walk along the country road to the Cleveland escarpment at Sneck Yate Bank. And from here, the route back to Sutton Bank lies along the route of the Cleveland Way – a really exciting walk that towards the end affords magnificent views across Gormire Lake.

The Cleveland Hills and the western moors

The most striking high-level walk in the national park is from Swainby to Roseberry Topping along the switchback route followed by the Cleveland Way. The heaving summits of Carlton Bank and Cringle Moor provide magnificent views over the low country to the north. Beyond them, the rocks and crags of the Wainstones on Hasty Bank (the most sizeable group of rocks in the national park and something of an oddity in this plateau country) make for a tough uphill scramble. This last summit derives its name from an old Norse title, but it holds a lesson for twentieth-century walkers – for many are the Lyke Wake walkers who have proceeded with too much haste over these hills and who have had cause to regret it 20 miles later.

From Hasty Bank, the Cleveland Way climbs to Botton Head, the somewhat undistinguished high point (1,490ft 454m) of the national park. It then swings north along the top of Greenhow Bank and on to Kildale. The view back across Carlton, Cringle and Hasty Bank is superb. The Way follows a track (known as Rudland Rigg) which comes in from the south and extends for several miles in that direction along a broad ridge between Bransdale and Farndale. If your taste is for a long, high-level route along which the miles can be ticked off at a smart pace, take a bus to Kirkbymoorside, walk the 18 miles or so along this track to Kildale (which is on the Esk valley railway line) and return by train. You'll see a great deal of the moors that way and much of the country that surrounds them. North of Kildale the country becomes more broken, but in some respects it is more exciting because here are the two prominent summits of Easby Moor – surrounded by conifers but clear at the top and with a memorial to Captain Cook – and Roseberry Topping. The latter is the most distinctive landmark in the North York Moors and keeps popping up on the horizon everywhere. It's not an easy climb to the summit; indeed, for many the climb up and back constitutes a good walk in its own right, and for them the national park office has recently laid out a new car park near the village of Newton under Roseberry. The views from both hills are, of course, first class.

South of the Cleveland Hills are huge sweeps of moorland on either side of Bilsdale. The panoramas in this area are now somewhat marred by the very tall TV mast, but the walking is still excellent. If you're fit enough to do it, a tough but very worthwhile walk to try is the Bilsdale Circuit (described in Michael Teanby's Dalesman mini-book – see Appendix). This starts at Newgate Bank, a famous viewpoint overlooking the lower end of Bilsdale. The route then curves north-west around the shapely and prominent summit of Easterside Hill, and thence north across the moors to Cock Howe. From these moors, the views over the surrounding valleys and across to the southern slopes of the Cleveland 'switchback' are all that a hill walker could ask for.

After taking in the Cleveland ridge, the route of the Circuit returns across the moors on the eastern side of Bilsdale, crossing Tripsdale ('a real gem', as Teanby puts it) en route, and eventually rising on to Roppa escarpment for a last view across Bilsdale and the moors. The escarpment here, incidentally, is another of the numerous striking landforms in the park. It is part of a line of hills running across the southern part of the park from Easterside Hill to Blakey Topping and Silpho Forest in the east. These hills – known as the Tabular Hills and formed from the Corallian rock series which is tilted gently to the south – seem to crouch on the southern slopes of the moors, overlooking them from a number of summits and ridges. There being much limestone in the Corallian series, the hills take on an appearance similar to that found in the Cotswolds away to the south-west, with their narrow steep-sided valleys, their dry stream beds and their prominent escarpments. For the walker, they add variety and unexpectedness to the scenery of the national park. For anyone based in the southern part of the park there is much reward in organising the routes of walks so that they take in some of this limestone country, as well as parts of the moors and fine valleys further north.

Rosedale, Farndale and the central moors

The 'fine valleys' referred to above are, of course, Rosedale and the nationally famous Farndale. Everyone associates Farndale with its wild daffodils, and there is no doubt that the carpets of yellow flowers which are to be seen extending up the valley for mile upon mile in late April are one of the great glories of the English countryside. 'Daffodil country' extends from Lowna in the south to Church Houses in the north. Anyone planning a day's circular walk in Farndale would do well to start at Lowna, follow the daffodil trail to Church Houses, and then strike up to Rudland Rigg to the west, returning by a moorland route. The national park office produces a leaflet describing the daffodil country and the routes to be followed.

Farndale is also famous for the battles that have been fought over the proposed construction of a reservoir in the valley. It was in 1970 that Parliament rejected plans for a reservoir, and since then the experts' estimates of our future water needs have been revised downwards, thus taking some of the pressure off Farndale. But how could such plans ever have been conceived in the first place? As Wainwright puts it in his book on the Coast to Coast walk 'It seems unbelievable that there are men with souls so dead, with visions so clouded, with appreciation of natural beauty so withered, that they actually scheme to flood the valley with water permanently. You simply can't credit it, can you?'

Like Farndale, Rosedale affords some delightful valley walks. In addition, Rosedale Abbey is a very good place from which to explore the central moors of the national park. A fine walk can be had by heading north from the village along paths to the open moor at Northdale Rigg, and aiming from there for the Bronze Age mound of Shunner Howe. Turn west here along the Lyke Wake Walk as far as Rosedale Head, and then turn south and descend a little to return to Rosedale Abbey via the track of the old ironstone railway. (A similar walk around the head of Farndale could be planned by starting at Church Houses, climbing north on to High Blakey Moor, following the railway track westwards and then returning along the high-level track of Rudland Rigg.)

It is the remains of the railway and the association with the old iron workings that are the distinctive features of Rosedale. Old mines and buildings are dotted around the slopes of the valley, and many paths in the area – notably the bridleway that runs along the western slopes past Hollins Farm – pass close by these remains.

Spaunton Moor offers acres of lonely open moorlands to the lover of solitude. A prominent feature on the moor is Ana Cross, which is one of thirteen crosses on the moors passed by walkers taking part in the annual Crosses Walk. This is a 54-mile marathon that requires no little preparation – the Long Distance Walkers' Association gives details of each year's walk in its newsletter.

South of Spaunton Moor are the lovely villages of Hutton-le-Hole, Lastingham and Sinnington. Beloved of tourists in the season, villages are of great interest to walkers because they can be used as starting points for excellent short walks in this area. Here the paths take you through beautiful woodlands, such as Spring Bank Wood north of Sinnington, and on to steep slopes leading to viewpoints looking across the moors to the north.

Newtondale and the Derwent valley

The gigantic glacial overflow channel of Newtondale has already been mentioned in connection with the revived Pickering–Grosmont railway that takes walkers to stations such as Levisham. From here, there are superb walks through the dale and the adjacent moors and forests. Levisham Moor and the Hole of Horcum are immediately to the east of lower

(*overleaf*) Farndale (Near Ewe Cote)

Newtondale, and one of the best walks in the park starts from the car park on the hairpin bend above the Hole of Horcum. Go straight down the bowl-shaped valley alongside Levisham Beck to Newtondale, north to Levisham station and then up on to Levisham Moor, returning to the starting point via Seavy Pond. The latter part of the route offers magnificent views across Newtondale and the high country beyond.

From the same starting point you can also strike east to the sugar-loaf summit of Blakey Topping – again affording views of a rare quality. This eminence, like Easterside Hill further west, is an outlier of the Tabular Hills.

The Hole of Horcum is a mecca for hang gliders, and their sport has caused many problems for the national park committee because of the number (and the behaviour) of the sightseers that they attract. The problem of how to manage such colourful spectator sports in a national park has yet to be solved satisfactorily. Part of the answer must lie in persuading the hang gliders (many of whom would accept this) at least to avoid holding the big formal events in sensitive areas like national parks.

On either side of Newtondale and Levisham Moor are the vast new forests planted by the Forestry Commission. As mentioned earlier, access on foot to these forests is more or less unrestricted, and this general access is supplemented by numerous forest trails laid out by the commission. Whether your taste is for such walks or not, there can be few walkers who would like to see a further massive expansion of the afforested land into the remaining moorlands of this part of the national park.

The Bridestones Nature Trail and the final section of the Derwent Way – both referred to above – are to be found in this area. The Derwent Way from West Ayton (on the boundary of the national park) to Lilla Howe (on Fylingdales Moor) offers a splendid route through the valleys, forests and moors of this south-eastern section of the park. It first passes through the exquisite Forge valley – a narrow, wooded slit in the limestone hills that is particularly attractive in autumn. It continues through the cultivated area of the Derwent valley near Hackness and then through a steep-sided afforested section north of the conical Howden Hill finally emerging on to the open moors at Lilla Howe, a Bronze Age mound which marks the penultimate major summit that has to be conquered by weary Lyke Wake walkers.

From Lilla Howe you can see to the west the 'golf balls'– the Fylingdales early warning station. The huge white spheres are, of course, quite out of place on these rolling heather moors, but they do serve as an aid to navigation that many walkers have been grateful for. But whatever redeeming features the golf balls may have, there can be no apology for the ugliness of the masts, wire fences and security roads that have been constructed alongside them.

To the east of Lilla Howe is a long, unspoilt valley graced with the name of Jugger Howe Beck. This wide, bracken-filled channel is followed by a public footpath that offers a most captivating walk. To verify this for yourself try the following route which allows a comparison between high moorland walking and a meander down this lovely valley. Take a bus or car to the point where the coast road is crossed by the Lyke Wake Walk, and then start by following the Walk westwards right across to Lilla Howe. This takes you across the Jugger Howe Beck.

Beck Hole, near Goathland

From Lilla Howe, head north down the planted valley of Blea Hill Beck towards Shooting House Rigg. This will bring you out opposite the top of the 'recommended' valley (actually called Biller Howe Dale at this point), and you can follow the right of way down the valley to the Lyke Wake crossing, and so back to the starting point.

Eskdale

Eskdale and its tributary valleys provide great scope for walks that take in woodlands, waterfalls and river gorges. The dales penetrate deep into the moorland plateau, and the long spurs of high ground that divide the valleys – Castleton Rigg, Danby Rigg, Glaisdale Rigg, and so on – make for exhilarating moorland ridge walks across heather, grass and bracken.

The 50ft (15m) high Falling Foss in the May Beck valley is perhaps the most popular of the waterfalls – the more so now that the Forestry Commission and the national park office have laid out waymarked trails in this area. There are also the waterfalls and woods close to Goathland, such as Thomason Foss and Mallyan Spout. These and other beauty spots can be reached on foot along public rights of way and there is the Historical Railway Trail which runs down the Murk Esk valley from Goathland to Grosmont and which was referred to earlier. In Eskdale itself, there are the charming East Arncliffe Woods, which cling to the steep slopes above the River Esk between Glaisdale and Egton Bridge.

For those with the energy to do so, however, the best way to appreciate this country is to follow a route that takes in both high ground and some of the paths in the valleys. For example, start at Glaisdale village, walk across the Esk valley by lanes and paths to Lealholm, and then climb up on to the open country of Lealholm Rigg and travel westwards along to the summit of Danby Beacon. This is a splendid viewpoint from which, on a clear day, you can see much of Eskdale itself, the broad dales on the southern side (notably Great Fryup Dale with its steep dale head), and the coastal plain and the sea to the north and east. From Danby Beacon you can head back across Eskdale to climb up on to Danby Rigg for a superb ridge walk around the head of Great Fryup Dale, and so back to

Glaisdale along Glaisdale Rigg – the route followed by the Coast to Coast Walk as it descends from the high moors into Eskdale.

For shorter walks in this area, and for an opportunity to learn a great deal about the setting and history of the Eskdale villages, a visit to the national park centre at Danby Lodge is well worthwhile.

The coastal zone

The cliffs and bays of the North York Moors are the most dramatic along England's eastern shoreline. Many people regard the coastline as the national park's most precious asset. It is certainly its most vulnerable. The pressures of holiday development make themselves felt here as in Pembrokeshire and Exmoor. Rich deposits of potash-bearing rocks have been found below the coastal plain and big mining companies have moved in to exploit these resources. Today there is one mine at Boulby, but fortunately, the big companies' plans to install huge mining complexes near Whitby have so far come to nothing.

The coastline itself is followed by the Cleveland Way, and this means that there is a continuous and generally well-marked path along its entire length. Strong walkers will derive great satisfaction from long walks along the cliffs – from Scarborough to Whitby perhaps, or from Whitby to Loftus. It's exhausting work following the coastline as it weaves in and out and dips and climbs sharply where valleys and creeks come down to the shoreline. But the walking is fabulous and the scenery is breathtaking. A walk from Scarborough to Robin Hood's Bay, for example, takes you past the narrow wooded creek of Hayburn Wyke, where the stream flows over a waterfall on to the shoreline; over the towering slopes of Beast Cliff, where there have been landslips on a gigantic scale; and on to Ravenscar, from where 600ft (183m) above the sea below, there is a stunning view of the gigantic Robin Hood's Bay. Here, the rounded sweep of the coastline is accentuated by the basin-like shape of the country immediately inland. The tumbling village of Robin Hood's Bay itself is a picturesque settlement of national renown.

87

So, too, is the fishing village of Staithes, further to the north. The coastline here is just as striking. The 600ft (183m) cliffs of Boulby confront Cleveland Way walkers with a tough climb but they also reward them with one of the best views in the national park. Not far away are Runswick Bay and its eastern headland, Kettle Ness – a smaller version of Robin Hood's Bay.

Along most of the coastal zone, the paths inland are plentiful and in reasonable condition. There is, too, the disused Scarborough–Whitby–Loftus railway line that runs close by the coastline. Although only a public right of way in short sections, this track is usable for long stretches, and you are unlikely to be stopped if you walk along it. The disused railway track and the network of inland paths and lanes offer much scope for circular walks that follow the coastline for a certain distance and then return to the starting point by an inland route.

For instance, start at Cloughton on the coast road by the national park boundary, and take the lane that heads straight down to the coastline at Cloughton Wake. Now turn north and follow the Cleveland Way down to Hayburn Wyke, then up along the top of Beast Cliff and so on to Ravenscar for the

Boulby Cliff, near Staithes – England's second highest cliff

superb view across Robin Hood's Bay. Then turn back, not along the coast path but along the lane that runs parallel to the coast about a quarter of a mile inland. This makes sure that you take in the views in both directions! Follow tracks that lead past White Hall Farm and Plane Tree Farm down into the Hayburn Wyke valley. At the bottom, pick up the path that follows the river as it runs through the woods towards the sea. Before reaching the coast itself, however, cross the valley and go past the Hayburn Wyke Hotel to meet the line of the disused railway. This can be followed almost all the way back to Cloughton.

7
Northumberland

The chief feature of the Northumberland National Park from the walker's point of view is the superb hill-walking country of the Cheviots. A glance at the Ordnance Survey map will show why. The contours crowd together up the long, deep valleys. Rounded, open ridges and summits radiate away from the central plateau of The Cheviot itself. Roads are few in number and the settlements small and scarce. With the Tweed valley to the north-west and the coastal plain to the east, the promise of fine views is clear.

The boundaries of the park extend far to the south to encompass the most impressive section of Hadrian's Wall. A 'walk along the wall', as it rises and falls like a switchback on the crest of the volcanic ridge known as the Whin Sill, is a unique experience. The walk overlooks country to the north that seems half-forgotten. Large, indifferent-looking pastures give way here and there to dark conifer plantations. The country has a sad and remote look about it. Indeed, remoteness is probably the predominant quality of the Northumberland Park. But it is not a remoteness derived from a sudden change in landscape – from low, fertile country to stark, desolate moorland (as is the case on Dartmoor). It is a remoteness born rather of a sparse population, an absence of heavy traffic and the fact that there is a safe distance between the national park and any large industrial centres. For the walker who places a high premium on solitude, Northumberland undoubtedly has a lot to offer.

In some respects, however, the park is a rather odd creation. Because it was designed to link up the Cheviots and the Roman Wall, it contains in the intermediate area what many people regard as rather dull land. It also excludes a large tract of mainly afforested country in the North Tyne valley that has been designated by the Forestry Commission as the Border

Hadrian's Wall at Walltown Crags

Forest Park. Although these oddities can be lived with, it is surely most regrettable that the national park could not have been extended north of the Scottish border to include the whole of the Cheviot Hills. As it is, the border ridge stands as the park boundary, thus excluding some of the excellent country to the north-west. Perhaps the English could give the Scots the Border Forest Park in return for their share of the Cheviots. The Scots would end up with more land, but it is an exchange that any English hill walker would surely rate as a bargain.

South of the Cheviot Hills, over a large area of moorland lying between the valleys of the Coquet and the Rede, lies a huge danger zone which the Ministry of Defence uses as a training area. The boundaries of this zone are well marked, and although there are rights of way over the moors, these cannot be used when firing is taking place and the red flags are

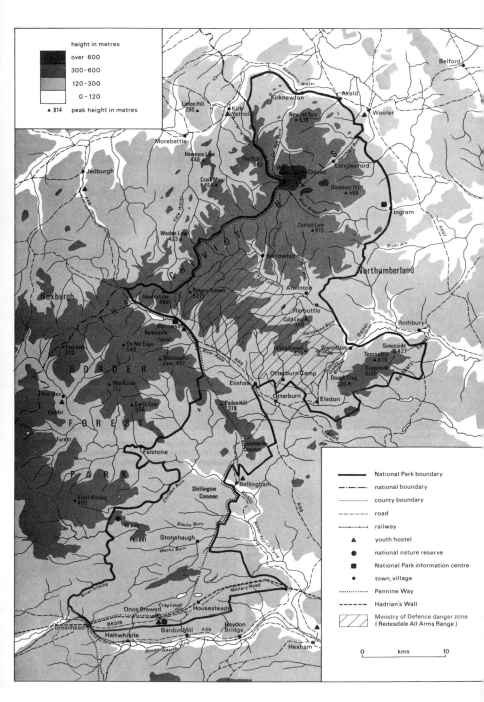

height in metres

over 600
300 - 600
120 - 300
0 - 120
▲ 814 peak height in metres

Belford

Linton Hill
280 ▲

Kirk
Yetholm

Kirknewton

Newton Tors
536

Akeld

Wooler

Morebattle

Hownam Law
448 ▲

The Schil
603

Langleeford

Jedburgh

Craik Moor
454 ▲

The Cheviot
815

Dunmoor Hill
▲ 566

Ingram

River Breamish

River Aln

A697

Woden Law
423 ▲

Barrowburn

Cushat Law
▲ 615

Usway Burn

Northumberland

Roxburgh

Ravens Knowe
527 ▲

Alwinton

Hungry Law
499

Harbottle

Cold Law
359

Rothbury

Byrness

Redesdale
Forest

Oh Me Edge
548

Blackmans
Law 457

Bushy Knowe
328

Swindon

Simonside
▲ 427

Tosson Hill
▲ 436

River Rede

A68

Otterburn Camp

Dough Crag
385 ▲

Simonside
Hills

Peel Fell
600

Elishaw

Otterburn

Elsdon

B6341

Monkside
512

Kielder

Earl's Seat
396

Padon Hill
378

Kielder

BORDER

Forest

Black Knowe
490

Corsenside
Common

FOREST

PARK

Falstone

Warks
Forest

Shitlington
Common

Bellingham

B6320

A68

Blacka Burn

Chirdon Burn

Stonehaugh

Warks Burn

River North Tyne

River Irthing

Military Road

Crag Lough

Housesteads

Once Brewed

Greenhead

Haltwhistle

B6318

Bardon Mill

A69

Haydon
Bridge

Hexham

River South Tyne

	National Park boundary
	national boundary
	county boundary
	road
	railway
▲	youth hostel
●	national nature reserve
■	National Park information centre
•	town, village
	Pennine Way
	Hadrian's Wall
	Ministry of Defence danger zone
(Redesdale All Arms Range)

0   kms   10

flying. Walkers seeking information about the firing should phone Otterburn 20241.

The final (or first) 50 miles or so of the Pennine Way pass through the national park, and this route links the finest stretches of the Roman Wall in the south with the Cheviot summit ridge in the north. The Way offers an excellent traverse of the national park. From the Wall to Byrness, at the southern end of the Cheviots, it crosses east-flowing burns and rivers. Here, the valleys are broad and shallow by comparison with those to the north. The ridges between the valleys swell up in huge waves and face the Cheviots. It is true that this central part of the walk is unexciting compared to the Wall and the Cheviots, particularly where it marches through dull plantations. But there is a feeling of anticipation as the Cheviots approach nearer and nearer, with a clearer view of them from every successive hilltop. There are also some delightful spots to be admired – the crossing of the Warks Burn for example, or, just off the route above Bellingham, the wooded path alongside Hareshaw Burn to the waterfall of Hareshaw Linn.

There are many special trails offering short walks and strolls in the park. They include some planned by the Forestry Commission – at Simonside (near Rothbury), Holystone (in Coquetdale below Alwinton) and Warksburn (near Stonehaugh) – and others, devised by the Tynedale District Tourist Offices, south of the Wall – from Bardon Mill (an 8-mile walk which takes in the impressive Roman sites of Housesteads and Vindolanda) and from Haltwhistle.

Walks on the outskirts of the national park – from such starting-points as Haltwhistle, Wark, Rothbury and Wooler – reveal the delights of the less dramatic country in the park – old stone buildings, attractively austere villages, historic remains and charming riverside paths. And almost always there are the distant views of the hills, the forests and the Northumbrian coastline. It is splendid walking country indeed.

The national park committee organises guided walks during the summer and these normally start from the main information centres and are led by park wardens. Details of the guided walks are available from the national park office. They range from tough hill walks to short 'walks with a specialist' that concentrate on the geology, birds and history of the park.

Much of the Northumberland National Park consists of either Forestry Commission land or open hill country. There is rarely any difficulty in gaining access on foot to either type of land, although there are the extensive Defence training areas near Otterburn already referred to, and there are many young plantations that are firmly fenced off and impossible to walk across. Outside the open areas, there is a reasonable network of public paths and trackways across enclosed land, although you will often need to use map and compass to keep to the line of the right of way.

Public transport services are good enough to get you to places on the edge of the national park without too much difficulty, but after that you are usually on your own. The Newcastle–Carlisle railway line stops at a number of places such as Haltwhistle just south of the park, and there are reasonable bus services along the North and South Tyne valleys and to Rothbury and Wooler. The national park office can supply information on bus services, as can United Automobile Services Ltd (United House, Grange Road, Darlington DL1 5NL). A special bus service operates in the summer along roads close to Hadrian's Wall and connects with rail and bus services at Hexham and Haltwhistle. In addition a 'midi-bus' service runs from the Once Brewed Information Centre to such sites as Housesteads and Vindolanda in the summer months, with a taped commentary given en route.

When walking in the national park for anything other than short distances, you must, of course, take the usual precautions. Perhaps the one point to bear in mind more than any other is the considerable distance from roads and settlements that your route may take you. As already emphasised, parts of the park are very remote indeed, and you should always allow plenty of time for your return journey. The weather can be very bitter, with cold, easterly winds suddenly bringing stinging rain or a damp swirling sea-mist. Walking on the summit ridges of the Cheviots can be particularly tiring, with the deep black peat-hags impeding progress. Don't be afraid to turn back if the going gets rough and looks as if it could get rougher.

The Cheviot Hills

The Cheviots deserve praise beyond measure from the hill walker. The ridges and summits – mostly grassy with occasional stretches of heather or bare peat – afford magnificent walking, with sweeping views in all directions. The open country runs deep into the long winding valleys and the fast-flowing streams run over gushing waterfalls in their upper stretches. They quickly widen to become meandering rivers, with clear waters running over granite boulders and pebbles. The bustling world is far distant, yet often in sight in the lowland plains on the horizon.

At the hub of the range of hills is The Cheviot – a flat, peat-covered plateau which would have no great attraction but for its height and the superb views that it commands from its plateau edges. There are many ways to approach it from the north and north-west. The long straight valleys of the Harthope and College burns run deep into the hills. The most straightforward route to the summit runs from Langleeford in the former of these two valleys. A path leading up the Harthope Burn valley past the lovely waterfall of Harthope Linn leads right to the foot of the black peaty summit (reminiscent of Black Hill in the Peak District). After visiting this, you simply head north-east along the ridge to Scald Hill and straight down back to Langleeford.

For a longer but much more varied walk, start at Hethpool in the College Burn valley and then follow the track along the floor of the valley to Southernknowe. Here, take the valley on the left, then follow it round through the narrow defile in the upper part of the Bizzle Burn valley and so to the summit. To begin the return journey, follow the Pennine Way along the English–Scottish border around the head of the College Burn. You overlook the great craggy cleft of Hen Hole and then aim for the prominent summit of The Schil on the border further north. Keep to the high ground as far as White Law and then turn down into the valley of Trowup Burn and so back to Hethpool. Altogether, this is an extremely exhilarating and satisfying walk.

Approaches to the Cheviot Hills from the east are generally longer, with the ground rising more gently than from the south

Shillmorr in Upper Coquetdale

or north. But a good starting point is Hartside, deep in the valley of the River Breamish. From here, you can follow the track to Linhope and then a path running parallel to the Linhope Burn to the waterfall at Linhope Spout. Climbing north, you attain the ridge that runs westwards to the summit of Hedgehope Hill, which faces The Cheviot across the Harthope Burn valley. Now there is a superb high-level walk around the head of the Coldlaw Burn valley, across to Comb Fell, and then round to Shielcleugh Edge and High Cantle. From here, you descend into the Breamish valley and follow the farm track down this winding, unspoilt dale back to Hartside.

To the south of The Cheviot is perhaps the most striking country of all – with the fells running steeply down into the valleys of the Coquet, the Usway Burn and the River Alwin. The ridges between the valleys can be quickly gained by stiff climbs from points such as Barrowburn and Shillmoor, and then followed north to the border ridge and Windy Gyle, or by turning east, to Bloodybush Edge and Cushat Law.

To sample this part of the Cheviots, start at Barrowburn and follow the track that leads north over Middle Hill and past Hazely Law to the border ridge. Strike across to Windy Gyle and then head south along the grassy ridge that brings you down to Rowhope. The views across the seemingly unending Cheviot Hills are superlative. From Rowhope back to Barrowburn you follow a deep and winding Cheviot valley that is so reminiscent of the remote Scottish uplands to the north.

Apart from the endless possibilities for circular walks in the Cheviot Hills, there are also a number of ways of crossing from one side of the border to the other. The trackway known as Clennell Street – thought by at least one author to be of prehistoric origin – climbs into the hills at Alwinton, follows a dramatic ridge route for a few miles and then drops down to ford the Usway Burn. From here, it climbs steadily again to the border and descends into Scotland at Cocklawfoot and the Bowmont Water valley. Clennell Street is joined at the border by the Salter's Way, a track shown on the Ordnance Survey map as a bridleway running the long distance from Alnham in the east over low hills and passes to Davidson's Linn on the Usway Burn. Many other routes across the hills can, of course, be devised. One of the glories of the Cheviots is that there is so much scope for planning your own routes and gaining the feeling while you are walking them that they have never been followed by anyone else!

Having sung the praises of the Cheviot Hills, it must also be said that there are fears for the future of this magnificent walking country. More and more, as you walk on these hills, you notice the steady expansion of conifer afforestation. Indeed, if the Forestry Commission and the private forestry companies had their way, most of the Northumberland National Park would by now be covered in conifer plantations. The pressure for afforestation has been enormous in recent decades – the Kielder Forest, which for the most part has been left out of the national park, is said to be the largest man-made forest in Europe. The rows of conifers, with their long straight fire-breaks running over the horizon, can be seen from almost every prominent viewpoint in the park. It is true that the Forestry Commission has opened a number of trails in these plantations, and some of them offer spells of pleasant walking.

But much of the afforestation that has taken place in the Cheviot Hills is heartbreaking – the grassy open fells have been clothed in impenetrable young Sitka spruce plantations that climb up the hillside in straight rows and have no sympathy with the natural contours of the land. In their later stages, these forests become dark and dull and have little or no appeal for the walker.

More recently, the park has been the subject of scrutiny by the UK Atomic Energy Authority. The authority has been scouring the land for a suitable area to use as a long-term depository for atomic waste. It believes that the deep, impermeable and allegedly stable granite mass that lies beneath the surface of the Cheviot Hills might be suitable for this purpose. The possible consequences are, of course, horrific. If spent nuclear fuel is to be dumped under the Cheviots, it will mean building works, drilling and road building in the heart of this still remote wilderness area. This threat has been and must continue to be resisted as strongly as possible.

The Simonside Hills

From the lean outline of the national park, an arm is thrust eastwards to the Simonside Hills south of Rothbury. These hills consist of a craggy sandstone ridge running south-westwards from the open moorland road at Lordenshaw. The hills slope gently to the south-east and present a steep scarp face to the north-west. They are a thousand feet or so lower than the Cheviot Hills and are quite different, being rock-strewn and covered in heather and bracken. Standing as they do in a relatively isolated position, they command renowned views over the Cheviots to the west and over the lowlands and the coastline to the east. Perhaps even more engaging, however, are the views over the valleys below – the secluded and unspoilt wooded slopes of the Grassless Burn, and the rolling valley of Coquetdale, with its broad, meandering river flowing down to Rothbury and beyond.

(*opposite*) Crag Lough and Hotbank, with Hadrian's Wall climbing the hillside above the Hotbank Farm buildings

There is therefore an excellent day's walking to be had on the Simonside Hills. The best walk is along the ridge itself, starting for preference at the southern end near Elsdon and climbing steadily to the principal rocky summits of Ravens Heugh and Simonside in the north, with views over Coquetdale opening out as you go along. The heather and the boulders make the going harder than in the Cheviots. Watch out, too, for boggy areas, particularly those on Boddle Moss, which should be given a wide berth.

For those wishing to take in the main summits as part of shorter walks, the Forestry Commission's forest trails starting from their very popular picnic site on the Lordenshaw road offer the clearest routes.

Hadrian's Wall

The most intriguing walk in this national park – perhaps in any national park – is along the Wall. In fact, the 10-mile walk along the Whin Sill from Walltown to Sewingshields Crags would merit a national accolade even if it were not followed by the most outstanding ancient monument in the country. The path rises and falls in great waves, often with precipitous dark crags on the northern side. Crag Lough and the other Northumbrian 'lakes' are overlooked by the path along its most impressive stretch – from Sewingshields Crags to Peel Crag. The highest point of the walk is reached at Winshields (1,230ft, 370m), and from here, as from many other points along the route, the views are very extensive, from the Cheviot Hills in the far distance to the north, to the Pennine plateau to the south and the Solway Firth and the northern fells of the Lake District to the west.

The path actually follows the remains of the Wall itself for much of its length. The remains of forts, mile-castles and turrets are also passed en route, and a little imagination, aided by some preparatory reading, is all that is needed to gain an impression of how things looked in Roman times. Standing on the top of Hotbank Crags in a keen wind and looking north over grey skies and dark mossy pastures, you certainly get the feeling of being on a lonely border outpost. The remote character of the national park is nowhere more acutely felt.

8

The Lake District

If there was but one national park in this country it would have to be the Lake District. Of the ten national parks in England and Wales, only the Lake District and Snowdonia are principally mountainous. Their highest summits rise to over 3,000ft (915m), and their dramatic, serrated landscapes testify to a recent period of heavy glaciation. The Lake District has the bonus of its famous and exquisitely beautiful lakes. Its mountain-and-lake scenery is unique, and the area has become a mecca for walkers from all over the world.

Here, more than anywhere else in England, one can only appreciate just how superlative the scenery is by leaving the road and setting off into the hills on foot. In many parts of the other English national parks much of the highest ground can be approached by car along a metalled, albeit sometimes narrow, country road. But not so in the Lake District. There are roads across some of the passes (such as the Honister and Hardknott passes – both best avoided in the crowded summer months), but for the most part one has to go on foot to get from one valley to another or to scale one of the many magnificent peaks that are clustered together in this national park. This is all to the good, of course, because it adds to the satisfaction of attaining a high summit to know that there was no other means of getting there!

It is appropriate in a chapter on the Lake District to direct the reader's attention at an early stage to the paramount importance of paying attention to proper equipment and to weather and ground conditions on the fells. Obviously, if you are simply going for a short stroll in the summer months through an area of woodland or along a lake shore, no special equipment need be taken, but as soon as you start climbing, the need for careful preparation becomes clear. Slopes are often steep and slippery, particularly when covered by frost or hard snow. Rocky ledges and ridges can be very precarious and the need for strong walking boots with a good tread on the soles is of great importance. At all times of the year it is essential to take wet-weather gear and an adequate supply of spare warm clothing. Even in the summer months, it can be extremely wet and cold on the tops. Take plenty to eat and drink – uphill walking in places like the Lake District takes a great deal of energy and can be very thirsty work.

Before going on to the tops it is a good idea to phone Windermere 5151 to get the latest weather forecast and an indication of conditions on high ground. Weather conditions are very changeable, and although the forecast is sometimes wrong, it is as well to heed its advice.

Never attempt a scramble or a rock climb that looks dangerous or is otherwise beyond your capacity. Be conservative in your estimate of how quickly you can move along; a mile on the map can take over an hour to cover if it involves a thousand feet of ascent. Always take a map and compass with you on the fells, even if you are following a walk in a guide book. Take the 1:25,000 map for preference – with that you are less likely to make a navigational error if the mist comes down and you have to steer a course by compass. And take a whistle and a torch – for obvious reasons.

Walking on the fells in winter demands even greater care. Snow and ice can be treacherous, and depending on the severity of your walk, you will normally need to take a rope, ice-axe and crampons – and know how to use them. It is best to go on a course and get instruction before venturing on to the mountains of the Lake District in winter.

Fortunately, there are no problems in gaining access to open country in the national park. Large tracts of hill land are in the safe-keeping of the National Trust (who, incidentally, provide the extra safeguard of keeping the Forestry Commission – with their monotonous spruce plantations that have so marred areas such as that around the Whinlatter Pass, west of Keswick – out of Trust-owned land). Many of the central fells are also open to the public because they are common land with a statutory

(*opposite*) Honister Pass and Buttermere, from the path to Dale Head

right of access. (Curiously enough, the explanation for this is that the fells once came within the territory of Windermere Urban District Council, and such statutory rights only exist over common land within former urban districts.) Elsewhere on the open fells, people are seldom denied access.

There is also a good network of rights of way. Some of these follow ancient packhorse routes, such as the one marked on the 1in OS Tourist Map that runs from near Grasmere across the fells to Patterdale, and even older tracks, such as the Roman Road from Penrith to Troutbeck via the long, straight ridge of High Street. Lower down, there are plenty of paths to take the walker across fields and meadows on to the open country. Many of these have been repaired and improved in recent years by local people working part-time for the National Park Upland Management Service. This scheme has brought benefits to residents and visitors alike and has been hailed by countryside managers as a great success. It is especially important in the Lake District to keep to the path at all times when crossing farmland. Many paths are used very heavily indeed, and farming operations can be seriously disrupted if signposts and waymarks are ignored.

For those wishing to walk the length or breadth of the Lake District, there are two 'unofficial' long-distance paths that provide admirable routes. A west–east crossing is described by Wainwright in his Coast to Coast Walk. His route, described in the guide published by the *Westmorland Gazette,* enters the national park near Ennerdale Water and runs across to Shap. It uses tracks and passes and runs through Ennerdale itself and then goes via Borrowdale, Grasmere, Patterdale and Haweswater to Shap. A comfortable crossing would take four days and this would allow time to make detours en route to visit summits such as High Crag, overlooking Ennerdale and Buttermere, Helvellyn, the third highest mountain in the national park, and High Street (2,718ft, 829m).

John Trevelyan's Cumbria Way runs from Ulverston to Carlisle and is described in a little book published by Dalesman. It is a south–north traverse which, like the Coast to Coast Walk, is mainly routed along valleys and across passes. It runs past Coniston Water and Tarn Hows to the Dungeon Ghyll hotel in Langdale. From there it takes the dramatic

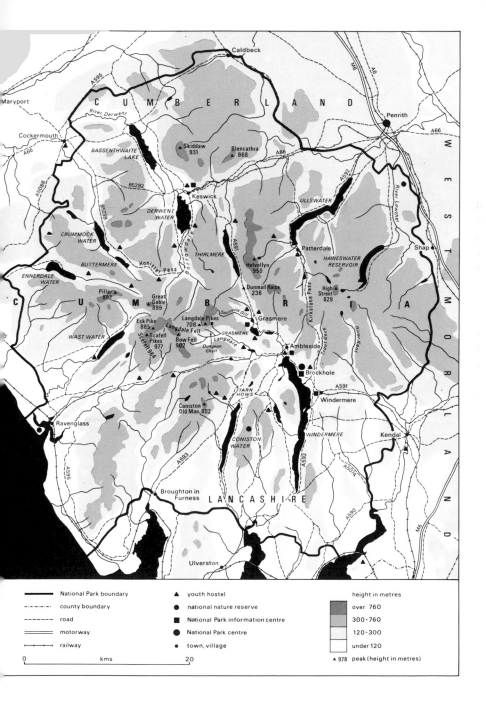

National Park boundary	▲ youth hostel
county boundary	● national nature reserve
road	■ National Park information centre
motorway	⬤ National Park centre
railway	• town, village

height in metres

over 760

300-760

120-300

under 120

▲ 978 peak (height in metres)

0   kms   20

Stake Pass over into Borrowdale and thence down to Keswick. There are alternative routes across the northern fells to Caldbeck, one going via Dash Falls, and the other, a high-level route over High Pike.

A 42-mile crossing from east to west (actually from Shap to the delightful coastal village of Ravenglass) is described in *The Big Walks*. It takes a similar route (in reverse) to Wainwright's, but aims to take in more peaks and follows, in its westernmost section, the incomparably beautiful valley of Eskdale, with its waterfalls, woods and castle (Muncaster).

In the same class as these long-distance walks is 'The Lakeland Three Thousanders', which is not so much a route as a challenge to those who feel up to it to climb Skiddaw, Scafell, Scafell Pikes and Helvellyn in one round trip, starting and finishing at Keswick. The 46-mile walk is described in *The Big Walks,* and the Lake District Area of The Ramblers' Association hold an 'open' marathon along this route every year in June. There is a limit to the number of entrants accepted, so apply early – and make sure you get fit beforehand!

At the other extreme, there are several nature trails and forest trails in the national park, with more being created, particularly in Forestry Commission land. A selection of the best would include:

– The Claife Shore Nature Walk (National Trust, 1½ miles); a trail through the steep wooded slopes overlooking the north-western shores of Windermere.
– The Loughrigg Fell Walk (National Trust, 2½ miles); a walk in 'Wordsworth country' that has marvellous views across Windermere and Rydal Water.
– The Silurian Way Nature Trail (Forestry Commission, 9 miles); a fairly hard circular walk starting at the Grizedale Visitors Centre. Pretty good as Forestry Commission trails go.
– The Stanley Ghyll Nature Trail (national park office, 2 miles); a woodland walk in a very attractive and popular part of Eskdale which heads for the Stanley Ghyll waterfall.
– Brantwood Nature Trail (private, 3½ miles); a most varied walk on the eastern shore of Coniston Water (open summer months only).

The national park office organises a very full programme of guided walks from April to October. There are many starting

106

points and many different types of walks. Although they are aimed mainly at visitors seeking an introduction to the Lake District, old hands can learn a great deal from them as well. The programme includes: Sunday morning walks from Ambleside; Wednesday afternoon walks from Skelwith Bridge in the peak season; full-day 'Discovery Walks' on various days from centres such as Ambleside, Keswick and Windermere; and evening walks from Bowness Bay and Keswick. Full details are available from national park information centres. It is advisable to book in advance for the 'Discovery Walks', for which a small charge is made.

Both the compactness and popularity of the Lake District have a bearing on the fact that public transport in the area is good. Fell walkers can get to almost any summit in a day's walk by taking a train or bus to and from their starting point. Trains run into the national park at Windermere, and a number of stations on the west coast and Kendal–Carlisle lines provide good starting points for walks or connecting points with buses going into the park. From Ravenglass there is the private railway line running into Eskdale. This takes you close to the waterfall country of Eskdale and also to within 5 miles (as the crow flies!) of Scafell.

Bus services operate throughout the Lake District. They are run by Ribble and Cumberland Motor Services and by a number of private operators. There are one or two post-buses and, of particular interest to walkers, a mini-bus service having the appropriate title of 'Mountain Goat'. This service takes you where no other bus goes – such as across the Newlands Pass to Buttermere. A 25p guide to public transport throughout Cumbria is available from information centres. Timetables need to be studied carefully to ensure that connections are met. Regrettably, services are much curtailed in the winter months.

Finally, there are a number of boat services. These are also referred to in the leaflet mentioned above. Some of them are particularly useful because they enable the walker to take a lakeside walk without having to return along the same path. For example, take the Ullswater boat from Glenridding, at the lake's southern end, to Howtown, halfway along its southern shore. Then walk back along the shore of what many devotees of the national park regard as the most beautiful of all the lakes.

Northern Lakeland

The fells and valleys of the northern part of the Lake District that are of greatest interest to walkers comprise the distinct block of hills to the north-east of Keswick which rise to their highest points at Skiddaw and Blencathra; the Derwent Fells and the fells around Grasmoor and Grisedale Pike, which lie between Keswick and Buttermere; and the valley country around Bassenthwaite Lake and Derwent Water (particularly Upper Borrowdale and the Watendlath valley).

The fells in this part of the national park are certainly of mountainous proportions, but in comparison to the more rugged and craggy fells of central Lakeland, they have a smoother and more evenly proportioned appearance. This is because the rocks of the area are mostly of the Skiddaw slate series. The central belt of fells is based on the Borrowdale volcanic series.

Looking first at the Skiddaw range, the most obvious walk to be considered is that from Keswick to the summit of Skiddaw. It is worth making first for the top of Latrigg, a 1,200ft (366m) summit that provides a classical and uninterrupted view of Derwent Water and Borrowdale. Heading north from Latrigg across a wooded col, you can then pick up the bridleway to Skiddaw itself. This is a stiff, steady climb which should not be rushed. The summit is a long ridge, and from it there is a view that is, in some respects, unusual for the Lake District. Skiddaw is not only a very high mountain, it is also a relatively isolated one and is set back some distance from the clusters of fells to the south, east and west. It therefore offers a panorama that, more than any other, serves to whet the appetite of the first-time visitor to the national park.

On the way down from Skiddaw, head for Carl Side, an isolated and rounded summit from which you have a view of the whole length of Bassenthwaite Lake. (Unfortunately, the view from this summit, and from Latrigg, also encompasses the 'improved' A66 road – an industrial highway whose construction was bitterly opposed by conservationists. It clearly should never have been allowed, but at least the controversy that surrounded it brought about today's official policy of building no more motorways through national parks.)

Skiddaw, Derwent Water and Catbells, from Maiden Moor

If Skiddaw is shrouded in mist but the lower slopes are clear, take a bus from Keswick to Bassenthwaite village and follow the trackway past the Dash Falls to Skiddaw House, a very remote group of shepherds' cottages. Then take the bridleway that comes down the Glenderaterra valley and end the walk at Latrigg, with its magnificent south-ward prospect.

The other major summit in this range is Blencathra, otherwise known as Saddleback. This can be scaled directly from the south, but the routes are rather hairy and should only be tackled after a detailed examination of the appropriate Wainwright guide (see Appendix). A safer and in some respects more interesting approach is from the village of Mungrisdale. From here, you head due west to Bowscale Fell, a lonely grassy summit which has much of the character of the quiet fells lying north of Skiddaw and bordering the Caldew valley (perhaps the quietest and least visited fells in the national park). There is then an obvious hill-top walk south to Blencathra (but one which calls for careful compass work in the mist). For the descent, head east across Scales Fell, along the top of the ridge, and then descend into the Glenderamackin valley, which winds its way back to the starting point and which will evoke memories of the Scottish Highlands for those who have walked in that area.

To the west of Keswick lie the Derwent Fells. The hills to the north of Grisedale Pike have been spoilt by afforestation, but southwards, as far as the Honister Pass (still one of the most daunting crevasses in the Lake District, despite the presence of a motor road running through it), the fells are high, open and glorious to walk across. Long, straight valleys cut into the fells and are paralleled by high, narrow ridges. The ridges meet along the length of Buttermere Fell, which overlooks the lake of that name. The opportunities for devising 'horseshoe routes' are obvious. Indeed, one of the most popular walks in the whole national park is to start at Stair in the Newlands valley, climb to the distinct little peak of Cat Bells, with its famous view over Derwent Water and Borrowdale, and then follow the long, straight ridge southwards, over Eel Crags to Dale Head, overlooking the Honister Pass. From here, there are various routes back to Stair, depending on the conditions and your degree of fitness. The shortest route is to descend directly into the Newlands valley from Dale Head, past some disused mines on the upper slopes. This track is a little tricky at first, but it soon becomes quite smooth. The first alternative is to stay on the high ground and head northwards along the next ridge via Hindscarth and Scope End. This is a particularly fine ridge walk, with a sharp descent and a superb view into the Newlands valley from the top of Scope End. The second alternative route – and the longer of the two – is to follow the track along the top of Buttermere Fell that links Dale Head to Robinson, and then head northwards along the ridge that comes down at High Snab. This is also a very attractive route, but it is one best avoided in wet or misty conditions, because the path along the top of the ridge runs close to the precipitous Robinson crags and on High Snab Bank there are one or two 'rock step' descents to be made.

Lower down, Derwent Water is surrounded by woods and steep-sided knolls and crags through which run a number of public paths. Much of this area is owned by the National Trust and so is open to the public. Many short walks of great beauty can be planned here. For example, from Keswick you can take a path that follows the north-eastern shoreline past Friar's Crag down to the junction of the Borrowdale and Ashness roads. Follow the Ashness road as it climbs steeply out of the valley and then turn sharp left to follow the path that goes over the top of Falcon Crag and Walla Crag, from where there is an excellent view directly over the lake across to Skiddaw and the Derwent Fells. Descend to Rakefoot and follow the path that leads north-westwards down to Keswick.

To the south of Derwent Water lies one of the most enchanting corners of the Lake District. Here, the valley of Borrowdale narrows considerably as craggy, wooded slopes crowd in on both sides. And a mile or so to the east is the lovely valley of Watendlath. Walking in this area is best done out of season or early in the morning. The aim, of course, is to avoid the traffic and the crowds.

A meandering route that does justice to the area is as follows. Start at High Lodore on the Borrowdale road just south of where the River Derwent flows into the lake. This point can be reached by bus from Keswick, or by launch along the lake and then a short road walk. Take the path that leads eastwards up the steep hill into the Watendlath valley. Keep on the western side of the Watendlath Beck and follow the path all the way up the valley to the village of Watendlath itself – the epitome of picturesque Lakeland. Then take the path over open ground to Rosthwaite in Borrowdale. Cross the rivers by tracks and rights of way to pick up the path that runs along the wooded western riverbank of the Derwent to the village of Grange. This takes you through the 'jaws of Borrowdale' on a low-lying route. As a climax to the walk, and to enable you to see from on high the country just passed through, cross the river and the Borrowdale road again to follow the bridleway and footpath leading to the superb viewpoint on the summit of King's How. Descend southwards by the footpath that comes out on the road near the huge Bowder Stone – a gigantic boulder shifted down the valley by glaciers in the Ice Age. From here, take the bus back to Keswick.

Central Lakeland

The central belt of mountains and valleys in the Lake District – from Ullswater to Wast Water, and from the Honister Pass to Ambleside – is underlain by hard volcanic rocks (lavas and ashes) that, in the western areas, contain granite and other crystalline intrusions. The toughness and variety of these rocks are reflected in the scenery. It is true mountain-walking country of a kind hardly found in any other part of England.

The eastern half of this belt of hills is dominated by Helvellyn, the third highest mountain in the national park. The most exciting ascent by far of this summit is from Glenridding via Striding Edge. It is certainly a route that needs to be taken seriously – indeed, it should be avoided in very wet or windy conditions. But on any fine day the main difficulties that will be encountered are the jostling for place and the incessant chatter of the crowds. So once again, the best advice is: go early or out of season. From the summit of Helvellyn, the best route is southwards along the ridge overlooking the impressive text-book corries to the east. This takes you over Dollywagon Pike and then down to Grisedale Tarn (one of the best spots for lunch in the Lake District!). From here, you take the old packhorse road that runs southwards towards the finishing point of Grasmere village.

From Grisedale Tarn you can look up to the noble summit of Fairfield, a fell that is at the apex of one of the classic walks of the Lake District – the Fairfield Horseshoe. This starts and finishes at Ambleside. First, there is a steady and straightforward ascent to Low Pike. From here, the ridge is clearly defined and you stride due north to the head of the valley and the two summits of Hart Crag and Fairfield itself. The return journey follows the parallel ridge to Heron Pike, with a number of minor summits on the way. The sharp descent brings you into Rydal village, with a pleasant level walk back to Ambleside along the Rydal Hall drive.

For those who wish to avoid routes that, like the two just described, are invariably very popular, the far eastern fells have much to offer. High Street is the tallest prominence hereabouts, and an interesting way to approach it is from the quiet and unspoilt valley of Longsleddale, on the eastern

112

Helm Crag and the Rothay valley

margin of the national park. Start at Sadgill in Longsleddale and follow the valley up to the Gatesearth Pass, from where you aim for Harter Fell. This fell stands at the head of the valleys leading into Haweswater – once a natural lake but now, and all too obviously, a man-made reservoir. From here, the route to the summit of High Street is clear. One of the attractions of this approach is that it is not until the last moment that the view across Hayeswater and the valleys to the west is suddenly revealed. If you have to return to Sadgill, retrace your steps towards Harter Fell and, just before you reach it, turn south along the ridge over Kentmere Pike. This is an excellent ridge walk, and it is one where you are unlikely to meet more than a handful of walkers. Pick up the track (marked on the OS map as a road used as a public path) down to Sadgill. However, if you have been able to arrange things so that you don't have to return to your starting point, follow in the steps of the Roman legions and head south along High Street itself to Troutbeck.

These east-central fells are high and wild, but on the shores of Ullswater they meet sylvan landscapes of superlative beauty. Mention has already been made of the walk along the southern shore from Howtown Pier to Patterdale. The route of this can be varied to take in some of the higher ground. A climb to the summit of Hallin Fell is particularly recommended, because it gives a view over Ullswater that should be savoured for at least an hour if justice is to be done to it. Walks on the northern shore are slightly marred by the presence of the busy A592 road, but one not to be missed is that through National Trust woodland to the waterfalls of Aira Force and High Force in the Aira Beck valley. This walk also affords magnificent views over the lake below.

Looking now at the western part of this central zone, one comes to the heart of the Lake District – Langdale, Scafell and the lakes and valleys flowing to the west and south. Here, as in the rest of the chapter, only a small selection can be offered from among the almost infinite number of excellent walks that can be planned in this area. The highest peaks themselves, Scafell and Scafell Pikes, can be approached along a dozen different major routes, each one worthy of a chapter in its own right. But if one route had to be chosen as a recommendation it should perhaps be that from Wasdale Head – after all, it is a sketch of this remote and famous location that has been adopted as the national park symbol.

Before setting off, remind yourself that the climb to the top of England's highest mountain is no ordinary fell walk. It needs careful navigation, a willingness to meet and cope with steep scree slopes, and no small amount of stamina. From the top end of Wast Water follow the path that leads up the valley of Lingmell Gill to Lingmell Col. From here, the track to the summit of Scafell Pikes is obvious enough. The summit stands in the middle of an area of monumental wildness. There is little vegetation, and all around there are dark crags and precipitous summits. Its twin peak, Scafell, seems only a short distance away. But beware – the safe route between the two summits is long and arduous. Drop down to the Mickledore ridge lying between the two peaks. Do *not* attempt to scale the rocks on the direct route to the Scafell. Instead, drop down a few hundred feet to the south to Fox Tarn, from where there is a steep scree scramble to the summit of Scafell. (Wainwright's guide [see Appendix] is invaluable for this particular walk. But, unless you have had climbing experience, don't follow his suggested route via Lord's Rake – it has become more dangerous since he wrote about it.) From the summit take the straightforward route downwards across Green How.

A strong walker can add a prominent feather to his cap by taking in Great Gable in the same day. But such a venture should not be underestimated. Although the round trip measures little more than 6 miles on the map, it involves over 5,000ft (1525m) of climbing. The route from Wasdale Head to the summit of Great Gable is well marked, but it includes some slightly hairy scree and rock scrambling on the highest slopes. However, the view from the summit over Wast Water is a just reward – it is undeniably one of the best in the Lake District. From Great Gable, there is a steep descent to the pass of Sty Head, from where the corridor route to Scafell Pikes can be picked up.

One of the finest ridge walks in this part of the national park is that which divides the valleys of Buttermere and Ennerdale. Start at Gatesgarth, just above the head of Buttermere, and ascend to the top of the broad valley on the right, swinging round at the top to the summit of Haystacks. From here to Red Pike the ridge dives and climbs like a switchback, with each new summit offering a different perspective of the valleys that lie hundreds of feet below. There is a steep descent from Red Pike, and then a beautiful walk along the side of the lake back to the starting point.

Away to the south stands a distinct block of fells that reaches its highest point on the Old Man of Coniston. From here, there are exceptionally good views across Coniston Water and the southern part of the national park down to Morecambe Bay. For an excellent walk along the main ridge of this range, start in Little Langdale and climb steadily along the smooth ridge running between the River Brathay and Greenburn Beck. This eventually brings you to the summit of Swirl How, from where there are magnificent views northwards across the Scafell range and the peaks that encircle Langdale. From here, there is a long grassy ridge to the Old Man itself, with the views southwards opening out along the way. A quick and well-trodden path leads down from the top to the village of Coniston.

The paths that run by the woodlands of Dunnerdale and the waterfalls of Eskdale offer delightful walks, but perhaps of greater interest to the first-time visitor to the Lake District are the lakeshore walks in this western part of the national park. There is, for example, a path that runs right along the foot of the Wast Water screes. At its southern end, this path can be tricky to negotiate, but further north it becomes much easier, and you can walk along gazing into the depths of the lake, wondering how this marvel of nature came to be created. (However, it may not stay such a natural marvel for much longer because, at the time of writing, a crucial decision by the Secretary of State on the future of the lake is awaited. For Wast Water – and Ennerdale Water – are being turned to as sources of water for industries on the west coast. Engineering works would have to be carried out to bring the plans into effect, and these would inflict considerable damage on these priceless landscapes. The outrage which these proposals have led to can be imagined.)

As for Ennerdale Water itself, it is possible to walk around the whole lake on paths and forestry roads. Likewise with Crummock Water and Buttermere, although short amounts of road walking are necessary in both these cases.

Southern Lakeland

To the south of the central fells lies a zone of the national park that is quite different in character – softer in appearance, lower lying and more wooded. It contains England's largest lake (Windermere), and this is the major landscape feature in nearly all the hilltop views in the area.

For a complete view of Windermere, take the path from Ambleside to the top of Wansfell Pike. To make a circular walk of respectable duration, descend on the other side of the pike along the track that leads to Troutbeck. From here, you can take the bridleway along the middle slopes back to Ambleside via High Skelghyll and the popular viewpoint of Jenkin Crag.

Anyone based in Ambleside for more than a day or two should also not fail to do a famous circular walk around the lower slopes of Loughrigg, taking in Loughrigg Tarn and

Rydal Water. Even by Lake District standards, this is a much photographed and admired area. Various routes are possible, but one suggestion is to walk from Ambleside to Rydal along the Rydal Hall drive and then cross the river to follow the path along the southern shore of Rydal Water. The wooded landscape here is utterly beautiful. At this point, the route follows Loughrigg Terrace with its thoughtfully placed seats spaced out alongside. A minor road then takes you over the pass to the track that runs just to the north of Loughrigg Tarn. From here, a bridleway leads you around the base of Ivy Crag and over the brow of the hill for a final and very attractive downhill descent into Ambleside.

Windermere itself is not well served by shoreline paths except in the wooded National Trust land on the north-western shores below Claife Heights. From the ferry house on the B5285 there is a national park waymarked route through the forests to the open summit of Latterbarrow and down to the famous village of Hawkshead. This walk is about 6 miles long and can be turned into a longer circular walk by heading back along the same route after visiting Latterbarrow and

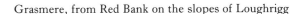

Grasmere, from Red Bank on the slopes of Loughrigg

descending through the woods to Belle Grange on the shore of the lake. From here back to the ferry house there is a lakeside trackway and nature trail, along which there are many points where one can stand (or sit) and watch the different types of boats go by.

Finally, a visit to a ridge that seems almost out of place in the Lake District can be recommended. Well to the south of Windermere town, but still within the national park boundary, lies Whitbarrow Scar – a block of limestone that presents a steep western scarp to the woods and valleys below. A convenient place from which to start a walk on to the scar is Mill Side, at the southern end of the scarp just off the main A590 road. Follow quiet trackways and lanes through delightful broad-leaved woodlands to a point just south of North Lodge. The path leads eastwards on to the open country above the scar, and you can immediately make for the highest point, Lord's Seat. From here, you can either travel along the top directly back to Mill Side, or turn off after a short while to take tracks through the plantations on the eastern slopes to Rawson's Farm and then follow rights of way back to the starting point along the foot of the cliff. In his book on the outlying fells of Lakeland, Wainwright describes a similar walk on Whitbarrow Scar and said that it was the most beautiful in his book. It goes to prove that there is an overwhelming abundance of beauty in the Lake District and that you don't necessarily have to struggle up 3,000ft of steep slope to find it.

9
The Brecon Beacons

The Brecon Beacons National Park is dominated by massive sandstone ridges and scarps that rise to nearly 3,000ft (915m) above sea-level. The three main ranges are – in the east, the Black Mountains; in the centre, the Brecon Beacons themselves; and to the west, the Black Mountain. Each range is made up of a steep scarp face and a gentle dip slope and, as such, is reminiscent of the chalk downs familiar to walkers from South-East England. But in the Beacons the scale is mountainous, with features such as cwms and lakes that are remnants of the Ice Age.

The Beacons divide industrial South Wales from rural mid-Wales, and the park contains elements of both. For the walker, this means opportunities for exploring wooded valleys and farmland that have never been touched by the Industrial Revolution, and also areas that testify to the industrial activity to the south – canals and reservoirs, old ironworks and railways.

There are a number of conifer plantations in the park, but fortunately, much afforestation on the hills is prevented by the fact that huge tracts of the open land are common land – you can't fence such land without special consent from the government. The status of the land as common also means, in practice, that there are no restrictions on public access. Some hill areas are also owned by the National Trust, notably the central and highest part of the Brecons range and those two peaks that stand in splendid isolation north of Abergavenny, Sugar Loaf and Skirrid Fawr. There is a good network of rights of way throughout the park, although their condition leaves something to be desired in the agricultural areas to the north and west of the hill country. Some rights of way follow ancient Roman Roads (notably the old road from Trecastle to Llandovery which runs to the south of the A40 and passes the

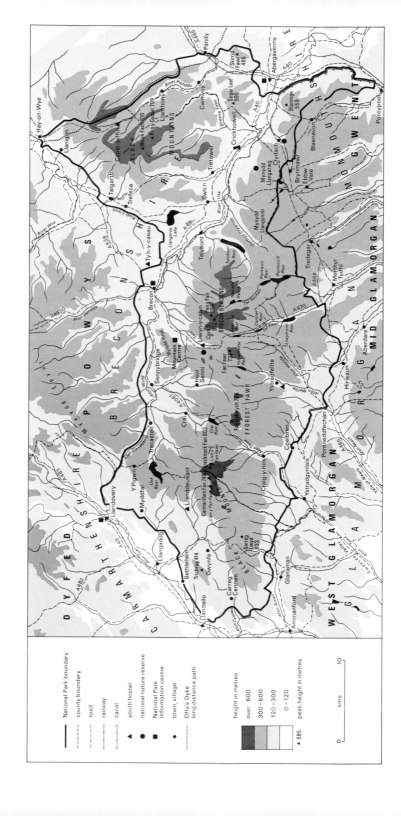

Y Pigwn Roman camps at its highest point), and old drove roads (such as the green track running north to Brecon from the Storey Arms at the highest point on the A470). The network of fieldpaths and tracks is supplemented by the 32-mile stretch of the Monmouthshire and Brecon canal towpath between Brecon and Pontypool. This offers some delightful, easy walking, with excellent views across the surrounding hill country. As well as being the only canal in any national park, it also acts as a natural walking route linking mid-Wales to the industrial south.

The canal passes through the former industrial centre of Govilon in the south-eastern part of the park. Here, there is a stretch of disused railway line (formerly running from Merthyr to Abergavenny), which the park authority has purchased and which is open for walkers, revealing some of the features of the industrial past of this area.

There is plenty of scope for short walks throughout the park. The park authority's own country park at Craig-y-nos, 6 miles north of Ystradgynlais, has 40 acres of fields, woodlands and lakes, and is linked by a footpath to the limestone caves at Dan-yr-ogof. The Forestry Commission has walks from Cwm-porth (recommended – see below under Ystradfellte section); from the Garwnant Forest Centre at Coed Taf; near the Talybont reservoir; in the quiet Sawdde valley south of Llangadog; and in the Mynydd Du Forest in the Black Mountains.

The park authority also runs a good programme of guided walks through the park at no charge (at least, there was no charge in 1982, but times being as they are, this may soon change!). The walks vary in length from 2 to 12 miles.

The only long-distance path to pass through the park is the Offa's Dyke Path. This follows the north-eastern boundary of the park, along the ridge of the Black Mountains running from Pandy to Hay Bluff. There are plans for a new long-distance path called the Cambrian Way, which, in its route from Cardiff to Conwy, would cross the park from east to west. The RA backs this idea, but it has run into serious opposition, and so it may be many more years before the Cambrian Way is opened.

As ever, Ordnance Survey maps are essential for walking in the national park, but there is also an excellent map published by the park authority on a scale of ½in to one mile, which highlights the main walking areas and the principal paths and which can serve as a first-rate 'route planning map' for the walker.

Public transport in the park leaves a lot to be desired – there are no railway lines, and buses in many areas are infrequent. Free leaflets on scheduled bus services in the national park are available from the National Welsh Omnibus Services Ltd at their offices in Brecon and Abergavenny or by post from 253 Cowbridge Road West, Ely, Cardiff CF5 5XX. National park information centres have details of other local services.

The Black Mountains

The Black Mountains are a detached block of hills, and are beautiful in their simplicity of form. The north-west facing sandstone plateau is tilted gently to the south-east and is dissected by long, straight valleys that run in the same direction. The intervening ridges, which rise to over 2,500ft (762m), offer magnificent hill walking country. A walk along the scarp face itself is perhaps the most exciting option in this area, especially as the views from such summits as The Tumpa and Hay Bluff extend for miles and miles across the lowlands of Hereford and Worcester to the east, the rolling country of mid-Wales to the north, and the even more dramatic Brecon Beacons to the west.

For those who are fit enough to try it, a 30-mile route which links up all the main summits in the Black Mountains is described in *The Big Walks*. But be careful – the ridges are relatively smooth and level and progress along them can be deceptively fast, bearing in mind their height. The real effort on this walk comes when you have to cross from the southern end of the western ridge to the easternmost ridge across three deep valleys! More sensible treks, which leave time to stop and stare both at the views and at some of the historical features in the area (the priory at Llanthony, the castle remains at Castell Dinas, etc), can be organised on the 'horseshoe route' principle – start in the valley climb to one ridge, walk along the ridge to the scarp, go back down the next parallel ridge, and then return to the starting point in the valley.

Sugar Loaf, Blorenge and the Honddu valley, from the Llanthony–Longtown packhorse track

A classic route starts from Llanthony Priory in the Honddu valley and follows rights of way eastwards up on to the ridge that carries the Offa's Dyke long-distance path. You head north along this ridge all the way to the scarp at Hay Bluff. The top of the scarp is then followed south-west to Tumpa. For the return journey one comes down the long ridge on the western side of the Honddu valley to descend through the steep wooded valley of Cwm Bwchel back to Llanthony.

A shorter route on the broken hills in the western part of the Black Mountains starts at Pengenffordd on the A479 road below Castell Dinas. You climb eastwards along tracks around this prominent hill and so on to the Y Grib ridge and round to the plateau summit of Waun Fach (which is actually the highest point in this range of mountains). Then you turn due west and descend into the main valley again to follow lanes and tracks back to the starting point.

It is unfortunate that not all of the Black Mountains range is in the national park. The park boundary was drawn to follow the Welsh border, thus cutting out one of the ridges and the Olchon valley to the east. Administrative convenience was held to override physical continuity, but in view of the large number of local authorities with some territory in the national park, it can hardly make any difference to add in another (English) one.

Although these hills are largely unspoilt, there is one particular difficulty that walkers will encounter in this area, especially on the lower slopes, and that is deterioration in path surfaces due to heavy use by pony-trekkers. This problem has been studied and discussed, and possible solutions have been advanced and experimented with for several years, but without any decisive progress. Some of the trekking establishments continue to attract their customers through flyposting campaigns in London, and they give every impression of being there to take as much profit as they can, whatever the cost to farmers and walkers. A stricter licensing system seems to be called for.

The Brecon Beacons and Llangorse Lake, from Mynydd Troed, near Talgarth

The foothills of the Black Mountains also offer some delightful walking, notably in the steep wooded valleys that run from the scarp face to the Wye valley, and around Llangorse Lake. The lake is very attractive and is set in superb surroundings but becomes rather crowded in summer.

To the south-east of the Black Mountains are two impressive outliers which afford half-day walks that cannot be matched elsewhere in the park. Sugar Loaf is, at 1,952ft, (595m), about 400ft (122m) higher than Skirrid Fawr, and also takes longer to reach from the nearest road. The views from the summits are incomparable, embracing the whole of the eastern and central parts of the park and extending to the Malvern Hills and the Cotswolds to the east.

For a full day's walk that enables you to savour the highly varied and attractive scenery of the Usk valley around Abergavenny, start at Gilwern and follow the canal towpath eastwards as far as the wooded slopes below Blorenge. Then cross the valley to Abergavenny, walk through the western part of the town and climb up to the top of Sugar Loaf via Llwyn-du and the ridge of Rholben. On the upper slopes you will be rewarded with superb views over the valley that you have just followed along the canal path. After attaining the summit, turn south-east and come down through the valley of Cwm Gwenffrwd to Glangrwyne in the Usk valley. The starting point of Gilwern lies a mile away on the other side of the valley.

The Brecon Beacons

In the heart of the national park is the most magnificent walking country of all – the Beacons themselves. The central ridge runs roughly west–east from the two principal summits of Corn Du and Pen y Fan to the plateau summit of Craig Pwllfa in the east. The walk along this ridge is fabulous. To the north are the huge, U-shaped valleys that evoke memories of the larger mountain corries in Snowdonia and the Lakes. The vertical rock faces that extend from the summits to the floors of these valleys add an awesome scale to the spectacle. Beyond, the land slopes down to the fields and woods of the fertile Usk valley. To the south are the moors, forests and reservoirs of the Taf Fechan valley.

The Beacons can be approached from the south, either from the Storey Arms on the A470 (for a relatively quick 'up and back' to the main summits) or, much better still, from the head of the Talybont valley, which is followed by a minor road. From here, an excellent circular walk can be planned, starting near the waterfalls above the Talybont Forest. Heading north-west, the main ridge can be gained quickly and then followed all the way to Corn Du before you turn south-east along the narrow Craig Gwaun-taf ridge and drop to lower ground to the south of the Neuadd reservoirs. The route along the main ridge climbs and drops steeply and frequently, and is quite tiring. At one point the ridge walk is crossed by a Roman Road known appropriately enough as the 'Gap Road'. This road is, unfortunately, used by motorcyclists and should really be closed to vehicular traffic at the earliest opportunity. I once encountered a group of 'trail riders' on the Gap Road and, not only did they make an insufferable noise driving along the track, but having once reached the gap itself, they proceeded to tear up and down the adjacent hillsides as if they were out for a day's scrambling practice. Motorcyclists are now being encountered in larger numbers all over the park (and in many of the other national parks), and it is high time that the authorities – who have powers to make traffic regulation orders and to prosecute unauthorised driving away from the highway – took a firmer line. If local authorities continue to ignore the problem or, at most, devise 'compromises' based on 'goodwill' (and in this, regrettably, they are backed by the Countryside Commission), they will find that the situation becomes out of control.

But back to the Beacons. Although the summits are easier to reach from the south, many people find that the various approaches from the north have much more appeal. Climbing south from Brecon, there are three stages to the walk – the first through level farmland; the second along the open, whaleback ridges that divide the north-facing cwms and offer almost daunting views of the summits ahead; and then third, a long, steep scramble on to the ridge itself. The disadvantage of this approach is that it's a long plod back to Brecon if that's where you're going – better by far to arrange to be picked up or to catch a bus from a point in one of the valleys to the south.

Pen y Fan from Y Gribin

Once again, super-fit walkers can turn to *The Big Walks* if they fancy a walk that takes in all the summits over 2,000ft (610m) in the Brecon Beacons range.

The area around Ystradfellte

Outside the three main mountain ranges of the national parks, the best area for walking in is the waterfall country to the south of Ystradfellte. Here, rivers flow down from the moors to the north across a belt of limestone, and there are caves, dry stream beds, waterfalls, crags, and other features typical of such country, to be found. The area is also richly endowed with paths, tracks, lanes and woodland walks.

A good starting point for walks is at the Cwm-porth car park just south of Ystradfellte by the River Mellte. From here, a path to the south runs close to the river (when it's not flowing underground), past a number of superb waterfalls and through enchanting woodland scenery. Shortly before the Mellte river joins the Hepste, the path climbs to the spur overlooking the river junction. The view from this point is excellent, extending to the Fforest Fawr moors in the north and down into the deep wooded valley of the Mellte to the south, with the Vale of Neath beyond. The path then descends to a waterfall on the Hepste river known as Scŵd yr Eira, which is thought to be the most striking waterfall in the area. Certainly it is the most exciting, because to cross the river at this point you actually follow the path *behind* the cascade of falling water, along the rock face.

At this point, routes can be followed either along the Hepste and over the moor back to Cwm-porth, or south to Pont Nêdd Fechan. From here, a path goes north alongside the River Neath and leads to further waterfalls, the best of which are on the River Pyrddin just upstream from its confluence with the Neath. It is well worth continuing up the Neath valley to explore stretches of the Roman Road which crosses from south-west to north-east and which, on the moors a mile or two north of Ystradfellte, passes the vertical Inscribed Stone called Maen Madoc.

The Black Mountain

To the west of the Swansea–Sennybridge road lies a vast area of open moorland that is distinguished by the fine ridge and scarp rock face that culminates in the summit of Fan Foel. To the north are the plantations around the Usk reservoir, and to the west is the castle of Carreg Cennen, perched on its limestone crag, and providing a focal point for popular short walks in this, the westernmost corner of the park. Between the reservoir and the castle, and below the moorland, lies a belt of quiet undulating farmland overlooking the Twyi valley. Here, the steep-sided wooded valleys, and the isolated knolls of rough uncultivated land offer a tranquil countryside where few other walkers are likely to be encountered.

The best and obvious walk in this area, however, is along the Black Mountain ridge itself. From the north, the ridge can be approached from the minor road south of the Usk reservoir. A trek on compass bearings across the open moor leads to the 'snout' of Fan Foel, which can be ascended by a track leading diagonally up the steep slope. From here, the ridge can be followed west to Bannau Sir Gaer overlooking the lake of Llyn y Fan fach (actually now used as a reservoir, but not noticeably so). The safest way off the ridge is to swing right round to the west of the lake and then head back north-east across the rapidly deepening valleys that drain away from the mountain ridge.

A more complete and satisfying route, if you can get the transport organised, is to start from the north-west at Llanddeusant, where there is a youth hostel, and head up to Llyn y Fan fach via the stony track used by vehicles obtaining access to the reservoir. The western end of the ridge can then be reached and followed east and then south along its whole 6-mile length, ending up on the Swansea road north of Craig y nos.

10

The Pembrokeshire Coast

The Pembrokeshire Coast National Park is quite unlike the other nine parks. It is much the smallest in area, and it is unique among them in consisting mainly of a long strip of superb coastal country – from north of Tenby to Cardigan. The park boundaries were extended beyond the coastline to embrace the distinctive upland block known as the Presely Hills, and a lovely wooded estuary called the Daugleddau.

Pembrokeshire offers walking country that is second to none. The coastline is followed by the Pembrokeshire Coast long-distance path – 170 miles officially, but probably a good deal longer, bearing in mind the rapid and frequent ascents and descents. The coastal stretches are dramatic, but also in part rather spoilt. By contrast, the inland parts of the national park are often quiet, picturesque and almost entirely undamaged. The Presely Hills offer fine country for hill walking (and, in parts, for bog trotting too). The Daugleddau is a delightful area for pottering around in.

The whole park is a paradise for naturalists. The spring and summer flowers add intense colour to the coastline. For birdwatchers, there is no better area in Britain. Appropriately enough, the national park emblem is a bird – the razorbill. The park also contains a great wealth of historic buildings and archaeological remains. There are stone castles, such as at Manorbier, hill forts, burial chambers and a most beautiful cathedral (at St David's). The rambler in Pembrokeshire would be well advised to read up on the antiquities along his or her planned route before setting off. Having features of this kind to visit en route – and there are so many of them in Pembrokeshire – not only makes a walk interesting, it also breaks it up into manageable stages, relieving the monotony of a continuous trudge and making the miles slip away without you noticing (well, almost).

Lydstep Point and Caldy Island

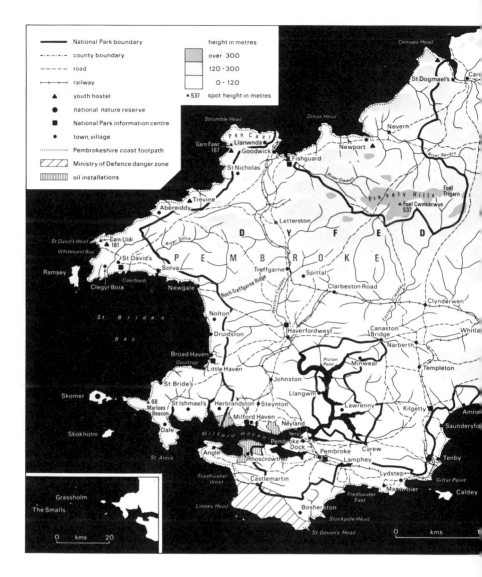

The footpaths in the park vary greatly in their condition. In general, the coastal path is very well looked after, but the inland paths are sometimes in a poor state. There is generally de facto access to the open country of the Presely Hills, and sizeable areas along the coast are owned by the National Trust, but most land in the park is enclosed and privately owned.

John Barrett, author of the HMSO's *The Pembrokeshire*

Coast Path, has said that bus routes in the national park 'are shadowy and their ownership is fragmented'. This is a common complaint in nearly all the national parks, but in fact Pembrokeshire fares rather better for public transport than most because, as well as its shadowy buses, it also has its railway lines – the main London–Fishguard route, and the branch lines to Pembroke via Tenby and to Milford Haven via Haverfordwest. All the bus and rail timetables have been brought together in a single booklet which is available from the national park office. A timetable of scheduled bus services operated by South Wales Transport is available from them at Cambrian Place, Haverfordwest, Dyfed SA61 1TW.

Ramblers new to Pembrokeshire soon learn about the special weather conditions that prevail there. Total annual rainfall along the coastline is quite low by national park standards – only about 30in – but there is twice that amount on the Presely Hills. Experienced ramblers will tell you, however, that these figures are underestimates, because most of the rain that is felt in these parts never reaches the ground – it is just driven along horizontally by the howling gales. The winds can be amazingly strong. They offer the best of reasons for not going too near the edge on a clifftop walk. They also explain the notable lack of tree cover in these parts. One lesson from all this is that, even though you will be travelling through relatively low-lying country, pretend that you're going on to the mountains and always carry well-tested waterproofs with you. Even with these, however, the rain is likely to get in and soak you thoroughly if you are out all day in it. Make sure, whenever you can, that there's a hot bath and drying room waiting for you at the end of the day, in case you need them.

But the Pembrokeshire climate has its compensations. The sunniest locations in Wales lie along the coast. Here, the wind clears the clouds away as quickly as they normally arrive, and with the heat of the day being tempered by a cooling sea breeze, this makes for the best possible walking conditions. If you can manage to do so, try to visit Pembrokeshire in the months of spring. The rainfall is lower than at other times of the year; the crowds have yet to arrive in their greatest numbers; and the flowers are at their most beautiful.

Apart from stormy weather, there are other things to watch

out for in Pembrokeshire. Coast path walking has its obvious dangers – there are landslips and overhangs, swift currents and slippery slopes. On the Presely Hills there are some nasty boggy patches lower down. But none of these is so daunting that it can't be avoided by a simple application of common sense and careful footwork.

For short and very pleasant woodland strolls in the national park, the Forestry Commission has forest walks of a mile or two starting from its picnic places in the Gwaun valley ($\frac{1}{2}$ mile and 3 miles up the valley from Llanychaer Bridge) and near Blackpool Mill, overlooking the Cleddau estuary.

The park committee arranges a programme of guided walks, running throughout the year. These are mostly short walks with particular objectives in mind – for example, to look at flowers and birds, or aspects of the history and geology of the area. According to the published programme, the leaders 'are all people with a desire to share their knowledge with you in a relaxed and informal manner which we hope will add to your enjoyment of the National Park'. A charge is made for each walk and in some cases it is necessary to book a place in advance.

One of the essential things to remember when planning to walk the coast path is to allow plenty of time. There are many reasons for this. The path rises and falls like a switchback and dodges in and out as streams and coves intersect with the cliff line. Some sections are steep, slippery or dangerous in other respects and should be tackled slowly. A strong headwind can turn a brisk pace into a ponderous struggle. And last but not least, there is so much of interest to see along the coastline, and so many superlative views to do justice to, that rushing along in order to keep up with a prearranged timetable defeats the whole purpose of a long-distance ramble. The Pembrokeshire Coast Path is most definitely a walk that should not be hurried.

The coastal sections of the national park

Amroth to Tenby

This sheltered, east-facing part of the park is unlike the other areas in being well wooded. Although the going along the coast path is quite tough in parts because of the rapid changes of slope, this section does not have the dramatic, windswept aspect of the rest of the route.

It is a part of the coastline that is heavily inundated with tourists during the high season, and is perhaps best avoided at that time. However, it is delightful in the spring and autumn. A good day's walk can be had if you take a train from Tenby up to Kilgetty and then walk back to Tenby from there. Follow country lanes from the station around 'Sardis Mountain' down to the coast at Wiseman's Bridge, and then take the coast path going south. You pass through some beautiful woodlands and, after turning past Monkstone Point, follow some striking clifftop paths back to Tenby.

Tenby to Angle Bay

This section of the national park contains some outstanding limestone cliff scenery. There are magnificent examples of all the features that distinguish this kind of landscape – steep, sheer cliffs and headlands, caves and blowholes, arches and stacks. There are, too, exciting stretches of sandstone coastline – much more irregular in form than the limestone coast, with more frequent changes of slope. And there are long sandy beaches backed by sand-dunes south of Tenby and at Freshwater West.

There is a very pleasant short walk of about 1½ miles around the headland of Lydstep Point, which is owned by the National Trust and which commands fine views over the sandy bay of Lydstep Haven and across to Caldey Island to the east. For a longer walk, drive down to the car park close by the remarkable hermit's cell of St Govan's Chapel south of Bosherston, walk out to the windy plateau of St Govan's Head, and then retrace your steps to follow the coast path north to the pleasant sandy inlet of Broad Haven. Cross this and follow the path along the top of the limestone cliffs on the other side, past the precipitous foreland of Stackpole Head and down to Barafundle Bay. After taking a rest here, work your way back along the coastline (here backed by the sand-dunes of Stackpole Warren) to Broad Haven, then follow the path that leads inland past the famous lily ponds to the village of Bosherston. Go south through the village and then take a left fork along a lane that takes you back to the coast path overlooking Broad Haven. Now follow the coast path back to the starting point, sweeping inland to cut off St Govan's Head. This walk reveals the extraordinary nature of the limestone cliff scenery and combines it with dune country and inland lakes.

To the west of Bosherston is a large area that is used by the Ministry of Defence for training purposes. When firing is not in progress, the walker can use the coastline lying between St Govan's Chapel and Flimston Down. To find out in advance about the firing, look in the local papers or contact the Bosherston post office (Castlemartin 286). However, a large part of the coastline west of Flimston Down (6,000 acres in all) is permanently closed. This is, of course, a disgrace, and one's sense of indignation about it is heightened by the presence in this section of the park of tatty holiday chalets, unsightly defence buildings, the remains of wartime structures and the giant oil refineries near Angle Bay. Altogether, this is one of the most abused parts of any national park, and the weaknesses of the system which has been unable to prevent it all is discussed further in Chapter 12. Fortunately, there are still some very pleasant spots, such as those around Lydstep Point and Broad Haven as mentioned above.

Milford Haven to Newgale

This section of the park is often rugged and windswept, but there are intermittent softer sections with quiet estuaries (for example, near Dale) and long sandy beaches (such as the superb and mercifully unspoilt Marloes Sands). The peninsula headlands of St Ann's Head and Wooltack Point are wild and windy and give magnificent views over turbulent seas.

There are short trails by Marloes Sands; around Marloes 'deer park' (the western extremity of which is Wooltack Point and which never had any deer as far as anyone can tell); and on Skomer Island, for which a boat leaves daily (weather permitting) from the little cove of Martin's Haven. Priority on the boat is given to people who have booked a place with the national park information service. It is well worth making a booking and going on one of the national park's 3½-mile guided walks around Skomer. According to John Barrett, the wild flowers and birds on the island 'composed one of the great sights of British natural history'.

The coast path does not lend itself to planning circular walks at many points, but there is an excellent ramble around the Dale peninsula, keeping to the path for most of the way. Start in Dale village and walk along the road that runs out to the Field Centre at Dale Fort. The coast path now winds its way in and out of successive bays, with views deep into Milford Haven. Finally, you reach the coastguard station on St Ann's Head and turn north to face Atlantic winds. The coastline is less indented here, but the cliffs are magnificent and you continue all the way to Westdale Bay, from where there is a short walk inland back to Dale.

At Broad Haven are a new information centre and a youth hostel at which residential courses for the public are held. Some of these courses incorporate coastal and inland walking.

Newgale to Poppit Sands
Newgale falls on the boundary between the 'English' and 'Welsh' parts of Pembrokeshire, to the south and north respectively. Ever since the Normans invaded nearly a millennium ago and held the south of the old county with their massive castles, there have remained different languages, place-names and churches in the two regions. More important from the walker's point of view is that there is also a change in the geology of the underlying rocks. The Carboniferous Coal Measures between Nolton and Newgale suddenly give way to much older Cambrian and even Pre-Cambrian rocks, with Ordovician volcanics and sediments dominating the coast between St David's Head and Cardigan. The northern coastline beyond Newgale suddenly becomes very 'Welsh' indeed – tougher and more uncompromising, with none of the wide beaches and estuaries found further south.

The coastline here is high, rocky and dramatic for almost its entire length. The section between Newgale and St David's Head is particularly good, being for the most part wild and unspoilt and under the protection of the National Trust. And here, along the northern coast, there is some good inland walking in the national park. Paths and open country take the walker to the top of the hills set back from the coastline – these include Carnllidi overlooking St David's Head and Garn-fawr south of Strumble Head.

137

Strumble Head and lighthouse, near Fishguard

The 3½-mile circumambulation of Dinas Island, to the east of Fishguard, is perhaps the most natural short circular walk along this part of the coastline. It is, of course, not really an island, but a massive round headland rising to nearly 500ft (152m) at its most seaward point. Start at Cwm-yr-eglwys go inland to the bay on the south-west corner of the 'island', and then follow the coast path all the way round to the starting point.

For a longer circular walk, start in the charming cathedral town of St David's and walk along the roads that lead out to Whitesand Bay, south of St David's Head. Now turn southwards and follow the coast path along the clifftop, parallel to Ramsey Sound, with the unspoilt Ramsey Island beyond. Then head eastwards, with the great sweep of St Bride's Bay to the south, and follow the coastline as it weaves in and out as far as St Non's Bay, from where there is a short walk along a lane back to St David's.

The inland sections of the national park

The Presely Hills

The Presely Hills, with the Gwaun valley and the Carn Ingli range to the north-west, are, apart from some bleak conifer plantations here and there, almost wholly unspoilt. They offer excellent hill walking, with views over the coastline and across to Snowdonia and Ireland on fine days. The hills are almost completely surrounded by sea and cultivated land, and you gain a great sense of freedom in striding across the heather and rough grass.

The Carn Ingli range, rising to over 1,000ft (305m) and lying between the Gwaun valley and the regrettably suburbanised Fishguard–Newport road, can be reached by paths and tracks from all sides. On Carn Ingli itself there is one of the best preserved prehistoric Iron Age camps in Britain. Indeed, the whole of the Presely Hills are of outstanding historic interest. There are exposed burial chambers on the lower slopes and, on Carn Meini, the volcanic rocks from which the bluestones of Stonehenge were taken.

Freni Fawr and Foeldrygarn, from the Presely Hills

Carn Meini lies along the 8-mile east–west summit 'ridge' (more of a 'shoulder' really) of the Presely Hills. This provides a fine walk and a relatively easy one for the well equipped. The route follows an intermittent hill track known as Fleming's Way, which is thought to be part of a prehistoric route linking inland locations with Whitesand Bay (near St David's) and sea routes to Ireland.

The Gwaun valley is especially quiet and isolated. The guide-books make reference to its ghost legends and folk-tales, and it's not hard to understand why this wooded and sparsely populated valley in the hills should retain such an atmosphere of antiquity. Although there are rights of way in the valley, they are not signposted and, to put it mildly, are variable in standard. The paths in the lower part of the valley, between Fishguard and Cilrhedyn are walkable, but don't trust your luck further up. As noted earlier, however, there are Forestry Commission walks in the Sychbant picnic place.

The Daugleddau

The Daugleddau is the name of that part of the national park lying upriver of Pembroke, adjacent to the estuaries of the rivers Carew, Cresswell and Eastern and Western Cleddau. It is an area that the park committee regards as its 'inner sanctuary', where the ancient oak woodlands, the farmland and the parkland are to be guarded carefully against the kind of unsightly development that has afflicted so much of the rest of the national park.

To judge by the condition of the paths, the land might just as well lie outside the national park, but at least walking along the quiet country lanes hereabouts is not so hazardous as in most country areas – after all, few of the lanes lead anywhere in particular. There are, too, the short trails at Upton and Carew castles and in the woods near Blackpool Mill, and for those with a good pair of wellington boots and an eye for the tide, there are some peaceful and fascinating strolls to be had along the foreshore in the upper reaches of the estuary.

11
Snowdonia

In many respects, Snowdonia overshadows all the other national parks except the Lake District. It covers an area that is more than three times the size of Exmoor. It contains no fewer than fourteen peaks over 3,000ft (915m) in height (even the Lake District can only muster four). These include Snowdon itself, which, being the highest mountain in England and Wales, attracts over 400,000 people to the top of its eroded summit every year. Fortunately, no other mountain in the national park is subject to this kind of pressure. However, it is a tremendously popular area, and in order to capture the atmosphere of solitude that is necessary for a full appreciation of this magnificent country, it is advisable to seek out some of the less-frequented ranges. There is no shortage of these; in the national park as a whole there are nine major ranges, and these can be divided into three groups as follows: northern ranges – Hebog-Nantlle, Snowdon, Glyders-Tryfan, Carnedddau, Siabod-Cnicht-Moelwyns; central ranges – Rhinogs, Arennigs; southern ranges – Cader Idris, Arans.

As well as the mountains Snowdonia has many delectable lakes, forests and waterfalls; a dune-backed stretch of coastline; and an estuary (the Mawddach) whose great beauty gave inspiration to John Ruskin and helped to persuade Rio Tinto Zinc that open-cast copper mining in the national park was just not on.

Snowdonia can also be a very dangerous place, particularly on the upper slopes in winter. In the chapter on the Lake District, it is stressed that careful preparations should be made before going on to the fells and that particular note should be taken of the weather conditions. Suffice it to say here that this advice applies with equal force in the case of Snowdonia.

With all the other national parks, including the other two in Wales, it has been possible to describe the routes of long-

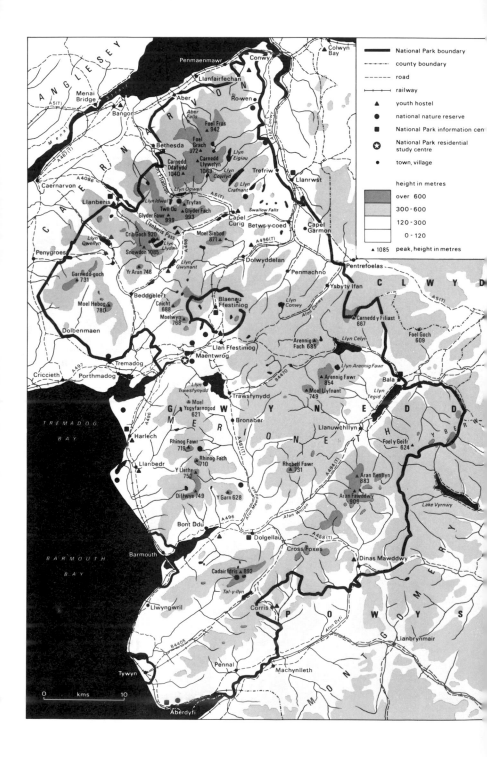

National Park boundary
county boundary
road
railway

▲ youth hostel
● national nature reserve
■ National Park information cen...
✪ National Park residential study centre
• town, village

height in metres
over 600
300 - 600
120 - 300
0 - 120
▲ 1085 peak, height in metres

distance paths that pass through them, providing clearly defined walking routes traversing the different types of terrain in each park. It is not possible to do this for Snowdonia, for the simple reason that there are no such long-distance paths. In fact, their creation has been strongly opposed. For, as the RA has found in promoting the idea of a Cambrian Way from Cardiff to Conwy across the highest ground in Wales, there is bitter resistance to the idea from the local authorities and even hostility from the mountaineers who have very exaggerated notions about such paths being artificial intrusions into wild and remote places.

But, *nil desperandum*; when no official route is available, invent one of your own. And for a high-level south–north traverse of Snowdonia, the best and most obvious route is from Machynlleth to Conwy via Cader Idris, the Rhinogs, Cnicht, Snowdon, Glyders and the Carneddau. It's a long, tough route of around 60 miles which, for comfort, should be spread over at least four days. But it's the wildest and most exciting mountain traverse south of the Scottish border.

By comparison with such a trek, it might seem a more modest proposition to undertake a walk linking all fourteen 3,000ft (915m) summits in the park. Indeed, it is a route that has now been followed many times, but for all that, it is a most demanding walk. The 'regular' route is described in *The Big Walks*. It starts at the summit of Snowdon and takes an estimated 11–13 hours in good conditions. After Crib y Ddysgl and Crib Goch have been collected on the way down to the Llanberis Pass, the whole sweep of the Glyders range is then taken in, from Elidir Fawr to Tryfan. The hapless walker has next to descend into the Ogwen valley only to be faced with a long steep ascent to Pen-yr-ole-wen and so along the Carneddau ridge to the final summit of Foel-fras. You have to be very fit for such a walk. In fact, it is much more agreeable to attempt only one or two peaks at a time and content yourself with reading the colourful description of a full crossing in Thomas Firbank's classic *I Bought a Mountain*.

There is a reasonable network of rights of way in the park, and these have at last been put on to a definitive map. The old county council of Caernarvonshire took over twenty-five years to publish its first map, and even now there are many rights of way that have not been included on it. However, the situation today is much better than, say, ten years ago, with many paths signposted and with the definitive map paths marked on the OS 1:50,000 and 1:25,000 Outdoor Leisure Maps.

Some rights of way are of very ancient origin. The track from the lower Conwy valley through Roewen and across the pass to Aber is marked on the map as a Roman Road, as indeed it was; but the prehistoric remains found along its route indicate that it was in use as a highway for centuries before the Romans arrived. Today, it offers a smooth climb for walkers heading for the Carneddau ridge, and it also makes a splendid low-level walk, with views across the Conwy Bay, for days when the mist sits heavily on the tops. There are also a number of old packhorse routes running across high and remote passes in several parts of the national park. An excellent example of such a track – and one that would appeal to those seeking real solitude in a part of the park where little has changed over the centuries – runs from Penmachno, 4 miles south of Betws-y-Coed, eastwards across open country and remote valleys to Ysbyty Ifan.

On open moor and mountain country, most landowners either welcome or at least tolerate the public having access on foot to their land, and you are unlikely to encounter any difficulty even when leaving recognised rights of way. Much land is now owned by the National Trust (for example, a large proportion of the Carneddau) or managed by the Nature Conservancy Council with public access allowed (as on Snowdon itself). For several years there was a serious problem on the Nantlle range (west of Rhyd-Ddu), but this now appears to have been settled by negotiation between the Snowdonia National Park Committee and the local farmers.

There is, however, at the time of writing, a major access problem on the Arans, in the south-east corner of the park. Here, the farmers have formed a protection society with the aim of barring access to walkers and climbers; they take a particularly dim view of large parties going on to this range. The RA is most concerned about this, because it illustrates that the rambler's ability to walk on open country in England and Wales is endangered for as long as it is based on the potentially ephemeral tolerance of landowners rather than on the law. The association is therefore paying much attention to the issue of access to the Arans. In the meantime, the advice to the walker must be that if you are going on to the Arans – and you couldn't be blamed for wanting to, because it offers one of the greatest ridge walks in the country – go alone or in a small party; find your way on to the open ground along a defined right of way; but come down if challenged and report the incident to the RA.

For those who prefer trouble-free walking of a short duration, there are an impressive number of waymarked trails in the park. Perhaps the most attractive are among those prepared by the Nature Conservancy Council. For example, in the national nature reserve around Snowdon, there are short nature trails on the lower slopes, starting at Pen-y-pass and in Nant Gwynant. In the far northern corner of the park, there is the Coedydd Aber Nature Trail, which passes through lovely woodlands to the impressive Aber Falls. An equally idyllic trail, of quite stunning beauty on a sunny autumn day, is the Coed Llyn Mair Trail through lakeside oak woodlands near the Vale of Ffestiniog.

There are several forest trails in the Forestry Commission's large estates in Snowdonia. The three main forests in which these trails are located are Beddgelert Forest, Gwydyr Forest (in the valleys around Betws-y-Coed) and the Coed-y-Brenin Forest north of Dolgellau. There are also one or two interesting farm trails; for example, the Gwern-y-gof Uchaf Farm Trail 3 miles west of Capel Curig on the A5 main road. This short trail has information boards along its course and illustrates the workings of a Welsh hill farm. There is, too, a farm trail with splendid views over the Mawddach estuary at Talywaen, a couple of miles west of Dolgellau. The national park office also organises guided walks in summer – a programme is obtainable from the park's information officer. In this context, mention should also be made of the Outdoor Pursuits Centre at Plas-y-Brenin near Capel Curig. This centre, which is run by the Sports Council, offers a range of outdoor courses, including walking and mountaineering. A course at Plas-y-Brenin is particularly recommended if you want to learn the basic skills needed to go walking on the mountains in winter.

Snowdon and Castell y Gwynt (Castle of the Winds),
from Glyder Fach

Public transport services in Wales have generally become so reduced that any walker without access to a car is, unfortunately, at a singular disadvantage. However, although it is true that many services have been cut in Gwynedd, the rail links to the area are a great boon, and highly commendable efforts are being made by the national park committee to improve bus services in the northern part of the park.

The main north-coast railway line takes you within close reach of the northern Carneddau, and its branch line to Betws-y-Coed and Blaenau Ffestiniog provides direct access to walks in the Conwy valley and on to the slopes of Siabod, the Moelwyns and Cnicht. Trains along this line run on a regular basis from Monday to Saturday, but on Sundays in the peak season there are special 'Sunday Shuttle' services which connect with Snowdon Sherpa bus services (see below). The other BR line running through the park is the famous Cambrian coast line, from Dovey Junction as far as the Vale of Ffestiniog. Stations on this line provide starting points for beautiful walks along the coast and into the hills lying hard by. The private line running through the Vale of Ffestiniog is another exceptionally useful rail link for walkers. Railway enthusiasts will know that there are two other light railways in the national park: the Tal-y-llyn line running inland from Tywyn, and the Snowdon light railway running to the summit itself. The latter is unlikely to endear itself to the serious walker and serves as a reminder of why some aspects of commercial tourism are quite inappropriate in national parks.

The main bus service operator in the national park is Crosville Motors of Crane Wharf, Chester. They have produced a timetable for all the bus and rail services in Gwynedd, and this is a very useful source of information for travelling by public transport in the national park. The national park office has launched a service known as the Snowdon Sherpa, which supplements the regular bus services. The Sherpa service buses run to summer-only timetables along routes that encompass the Snowdon massif (ie around a triangle based on Caernarfon, Pen-y-Gwryd and Beddgelert), with extensions to Llanrwst in the Conwy valley and to Porthmadog. They are designed to provide a service for people who want either to leave their car at home or to take it to one point, then walk to another point on

148

a bus route and catch the bus back. As a matter of fact, it is often difficult to find a parking spot on the roads around Snowdon in the peak months, and it therefore makes a lot of sense to go by bus instead. A timetable for the Sherpa buses (which can, incidentally, be stopped on request at any point) is obtainable from the national park information officer.

The northern ranges

The highest, most dramatic and most popular ranges are in the northern part of the national park. For views of Snowdon itself and for hill walks requiring slightly less exertion than the ascents of the 3,000ft plus (915m plus) peaks, head for Moel Hebog, near Beddgelert, or Cnicht above Cwm Croesor. But if you are visiting Snowdonia for the first time and want to sample the best it can offer, you will want to make for the Carneddau, Glyders and Snowdon.

If blessed with a good day, a walk along the full length of the Carneddau ridge can be a most exhilarating and fulfilling experience. A favourite starting place is Llanfairfechan on the north coast. From here, you head up the valley, south-eastwards towards the pass of Bwlch y Ddeufaen on the old Roman Road. The main ridge climbs steadily to the south. An alternative and more attractive approach is from Aber. After passing through unspoilt natural woodlands, you reach the Aber Falls. Above the falls, you climb steeply across the wind-swept hills to the summit of Foel-fras on the main ridge. From here, the walk along the ridge reveals views of increasing drama – grassy slopes give way to precipitous crags; mountain tarns are seen nestling hundreds of feet below at the foot of sheer drops. By the time you arrive at the rocky summit of the highest peak, Carnedd Llywelyn, you feel that the mountains of Snowdonia have been well and truly reached at last. As views go, however, the best is yet to come. From Carnedd Dafydd the outlines of the Glyder range become clear; and from Pan-yr-ole-wen there is a spectacular view over Llyn Ogwen directly below, across to Llyn Idwal lying in its gigantic mountain basin, and beyond to the clearly defined summits of Tryfan and the Glyders.

An ascent of the last-mentioned peaks is a mountain walk

par excellence. But if you haven't been on them before, don't attempt the ascent unless in the company of someone with experience of these mountains. They are not dangerous in the sense of requiring rock-climbing skills, but they do need to be treated with more than the usual degree of caution and respect. Also, keep to the well-trodden tracks on a first ascent. Starting from Llyn Ogwen, the safest and easiest route to the summit of Tryfan is via Llyn Bochlwyd to the col between Tryfan and the Glyders known as Bwlch Tryfan. Here you turn left to follow the track to the summit. The more popular route, however, is along the north ridge starting near the head of Llyn Ogwen. Poucher (see Appendix) describes this route appropriately as a 'sporting course', and you must certainly be prepared for a lot of scrambling and the proximity of steep rocky slopes on both sides. Either way, the route from Tryfan to the Glyders lies to the north from Bwlch Tryfan again. To gain the summit of Glyder Fach by this route you must ascend Bristly Ridge, and this involves a lot of technically easy rock climbing which if tackled carefully, should present no serious problem to a moderately experienced hill walker. However, if you feel this is beyond your capacity, plan an alternative route which misses out Tryfan and Bristly Ridge altogether – for example, by starting from Capel Curig and climbing steadily westwards along the ridge leading to the Glyders. Alternatively, start from Pen-y-Gwryd to the south and follow the well-used, albeit rather wet, route to the top known as the Miners' Track. Once reached, the summits of Glyder Fach and Glyder Fawr will be found to consist of a most striking and weird expanse of stones, rock slabs and boulders. The views are quite breathtaking too!

Round off the walk with a climb to Y Garn, further to the north along the main ridge. From this point, you can see nearly all the principal summits of the 3,000ft (915m) mountains – the Snowdon massif to the south, the Glyders and Tryfan to the east, and the Carneddau to the north. There is a relatively straightforward descent from this summit down the ridge leading back to Llyn Ogwen.

(*opposite*) Y Lliwedd, the south-east ridge of Snowdon, from Bwlch y Saethau (Pass of the Arrows)

As for Snowdon itself, there is no shortage of tracks leading to its summit and on almost any day of the year, but particularly in the summer months, large numbers of other walkers are likely to be encountered. If tackling Snowdon for the first time, a good route to choose is the Llanberis Path, which follows a similar route to the summit as that taken by the railway. The path climbs steadily, and the splendours of this indubitably magnificent mountain are slowly revealed. As a variation on the more usual routes for descent, head south towards the outlying peak of Yr Aran. From the (usually quiet) top of this hill, there is an unrivalled view of the southern flanks of Snowdon; and also, to the south, the valley of Nantgwynant, with its woods and lakes; and beyond to the unmistakable summits of Hebog and Cnicht. From Yr Aran you can descend either along the south-west ridge to Beddgelert or along the eastern ridge into Nantgwynant.

There is no lack of beautiful lowland country in which to walk when conditions on the tops make mountain walks unpleasant or inadvisable. Notable beauty spots are the Conwy

Llanberis Pass, from the lower part of the 'Pyg' track up Snowdon. The camera is looking down the wildest valley in Wales towards Llanberis and the slate quarries on the slopes of the mountain Elidir Fawr. On the right is Esgaire Felen, south-west shoulder of Glyder Fawr

valley just above Betws-ys-Coed, the Pass of Aberglaslyn and the Vale of Ffestiniog. A famous walk in the Conwy valley is along the track of the old London road from Beaver Pool, where the A470 crosses the River Conwy. The track runs just below the A5, overlooking the river and with the craggy eminence of Dinas Mawr towering above. You can descend to the pools of the so-called Fairy Glen and glance over the Conwy and Machno falls before returning on the other side of the river along a forest road.

The Pass of Aberglaslyn, another renowned river gorge, lies south of Beddgelert, from where you can walk to the gorge along the line of a disused railway on the eastern side of the pass. For an attractive return journey, follow the small valley of Cwn Bychan to its head and then traverse the north-facing scarp on the other side back to Beddgelert.

Finally, it would be difficult to recommend too highly some walking in the Vale of Ffestiniog. The woodlands thereabouts are exquisite. You can walk, for example, from the Dduallt halt on the Ffestiniog railway along footpaths and trackways through National Trust woodland to Llyn Mair, and perhaps follow this, by a stroll through the grounds of Plas Tan-y-bwlch. This is a residential study centre owned by the national park committee, and attached to it are 105 acres of woodland and garden that are open to the public in the summer months.

The central ranges

The central ranges of Snowdonia extend from the sandy beaches along the Cambrian coast, across the daunting heights of the Rhinogs and past the massively incongruous nuclear power station at Trawsfynydd to the isolated Arennig mountains overlooking the secluded reservoir of Llyn Celyn. By contrast with the northern ranges, some of which are being climbed by thousands of puffing and chattering walkers on a fine day, these hills in the central part of the national park are usually quiet and remote. In the case of the Rhinogs, there is an added element of truly untamed wildness which vests them with a unique and indeed slightly dangerous quality. Here the ground is broken, uneven and strewn with rocks and boulders of all shapes and sizes, and the heather vegetation clings precariously to the soil lying thinly on the rock below.

A complete traverse of the Rhinog ridge from Trawsfynydd to Barmouth is much more arduous than its distance on the map (just over 20 miles) would indicate. It is described in *The Big Walks* but should not really be attempted until some walking has already been done in the area. The most straightforward and perhaps most satisfying walk in the range is the ascent of Rhinog Fawr from Cwm Bychan via the so-called Roman Steps (now thought to be of medieval origin). The summit commands the most magnificent view across Snowdon and the northern ranges, but getting to it involves some tiring work ascending crags, boulders and steep heather slopes. Return by the same route, being very careful not to twist your ankle by catching a foot between rocks hidden by vegetation.

By contrast, the ascent of Arennig Fawr, 12 miles to the east, is a simple affair. From a point on the B4391 Bala road just above the head of Lyn Celyn, there is a path that takes you across to the other side of the valley. From here, you follow a track around the eastern shores of Llyn Arennig Fawr and so on to the summit via a broad open ridge. If you have a good day, take in Arennig Fawr in the morning, enjoy lunch at the picnic site at the head of the lake, and then scale Arennig Fach in the afternoon (start on the B4391 at about GR 830400 and aim first for the outlying shoulder of Y Foel). These two mountains, being in an isolated position in the middle of the park, command views of many other Snowdonia ranges – the Snowdon massif to the north-west; the broken skyline of the Rhinogs to the west; and the prominent peaks of the Arans to the south.

As in the northern part of the national park, there are in this central zone some outstandingly attractive walks on the lower slopes as well. For example, there is a view from Moel Goedog (GR 613325) that Showell Styles has called 'the finest panoramic view in all Wales'. It embraces the dunes of Morfa Harlech below, the long westward sweep of the Lleyn peninsula coastline, and the mountains of Snowdon and its satellites. However, getting to this point is not an entirely straightforward affair, because the paths in this area – although many on the map – are often hard to trace on the ground. Take the Outdoor Leisure Map and a compass, but also pick a quiet day out of season, so that if you decide to keep mainly to the country roads instead, you won't be dogged by traffic too much. A very pleasant circular walk can be had by starting at Harlech and heading south-east by lanes and paths over into the lovely wooded valley of the Afon Artro. At the head of the valley the country opens out, and you can take a track up to Cwm-mawr and then westwards across the ridge to the afore-mentioned Moel Goedog to feast on the view. Return to Harlech by country roads or along footpaths and bridleways.

To the south, you can now walk along almost the whole length of the southern shore of the Mawddach estuary by fol-lowing the trail laid out by the national park office along the disused railway line from Penmaenpool to Morfa Mawddach. At Arthog, it is definitely worth leaving this trail and heading south along the path running up a wooded valley, past a water-fall, to the high ground which overlooks the estuary. Nestling in these foothills are the National Trust lakes of Llynnau Cre-gennen and it is a beautiful spot at which to rest after a good walk.

Finally, mention must certainly be made of the well-known Precipice Walk. This starts near a country lane north of Dol-gellau (at roughly GR 745213) and runs for 3 miles at the 800ft (244m) contour around a ridge with superb and justly famous views over the estuary, the afforested mountains to the north and the great bulk of Cader Idris to the south. It is a walk which justifies the theory held by many walkers that the best part of a walk is often on the middle slopes.

The southern ranges

As mountains go, Cader Idris is a real giant. Although its summit does not quite reach 3,000ft (915m), it stands there proud and unrivalled, surrounded on almost all sides by stu-pendously deep dark precipices and towering above the Mawddach estuary on one side and the perfectly shaped glacial trough of Tal-y-llyn on the other. And yet the walker can ascend it with no technical difficulty. Its slopes inspire awe rather than fear, and there is no need to offer the same warnings about Cader as have been necessary about, say, Tryfan and Bristly Ridge.

155

The best of several excellent routes to the summit is from the south-east, starting near the Tal-y-llyn lake. Take a bus from Dolgellau round to Minffordd and start at the nearby footpath leading up into the steep wooded slopes at the foot of the mountain. You soon emerge into wild mountainous country, making for the shores of Llyn Cau which lies at the foot of one of the largest and most magnificent corries in the national park. The route to the summit lies along the path that encircles this gigantic hollow, climbing first along the southern ridge of Craig Lwyd and then turning northwards to Craig Cau and the top. One of the great appeals of this approach is the emergence, as you reach the highest slopes, of the incredible view to the north, with the estuary below and, beyond it, the Rhinogs and Snowdon. From the summit, the best route back to Dolgellau is eastwards right along the summit ridge to Gau Graig, descending along the track that runs around the tip of this ridge down to Bwlch-coch and on to Dolgellau.

The other major range in this southern part of the park is the Arans. Reference has already been made to the access problem which exists here, but on the assumption that this will eventually be resolved, a recommended route on to the long, east-facing ridge is as follows. Take the right of way that runs from the Bala–Dolgellau road south-eastwards across the valley and up through the forestry plantations to the top of the Craig y Ffynnon pass. From here, head northwards along the main ridge to the summits of Aran Fawddwy and Aran Benllyn. The ridge descends smoothly towards Llanuwchllyn, and you should pick up the bridleway that runs along the western slopes of the ridge down to the road leading through the village.

The character of the hill country to the west and south-west of Cader Idris, in the southernmost corner of the national park, is in sharp contrast to that of Cader and the other mountains of Snowdonia, with its secluded wooded valleys and smooth rounded ridges. There is a fine walk along the 800ft (244m) ridge running between the Dyfi estuary to the south and Happy Valley to the north. It can be reached from several

(*opposite*) The Ganllwyd valley, near Dolgellau

points on the Tywyn–Machynlleth road, but it is best walked from the east. Start about a mile south-west of Cwrt and then walk all the way along the top back to the coast road at a point close by the mouth of the Dyfi estuary, in the far south-western corner of the national park.

12
National Parks –
Their Past and Their Future

The reader of the preceding chapters will have become aware that, although there is much fine and beautiful walking country in our national parks, they are by no means without their scars and intrusions. Nor are facilities for public access all that could be wished for in some areas. The concept of national parks in this country clearly commands strong public support, but the imperfections of the system are all too clear.

As mentioned in the Introduction, the ten national parks of England and Wales were designated in the 1950s. They were set up under the National Parks and Access to the Countryside Act 1949, a piece of legislation that had long been fought for by the Ramblers' Association and other conservation bodies. (For a much more detailed examination of the history of this Act and the campaigns that led up to it see *Right to Roam* by Tom Stephenson (David & Charles, in preparation) and *Peacetime History, Environmental Planning Volume II–National Parks and Recreation in the Countryside* by G. E. Cherry (HMSO, 1975).) However, the Act was regarded by the RA as having some key weaknesses. It provided for national parks to be administered by independent planning boards – bodies that had their own powers and funds and that were tailor-made for carrying out the statutory duties of conserving natural beauty and promoting public access. But the Act contained a loophole. The minister was given the power to rule out the creation of a board if he thought that circumstances warranted it. The outcome was that, after boards had been set up for the Peak District and the Lake District, the government pulled down the shutters and prevented the creation of any more. Instead, the administration of national parks was left entirely in the hands of the local authorities, many of whom had strongly opposed the designation of these parks in the first place. Advisory committees with national representation were established for each park, but their influence was marginal and they certainly had no power to prevent intrusive, large-scale developments such as nuclear power stations, major quarries and oil refineries.

The sequel was much as predicted by the RA. The boards tackled their job with diligence and their efforts were attended by much success. This was particularly notable in the Peak District, where large areas of moorland were opened to the public following the conclusion of access agreements, and where the highest standards of rural conservation were established. But in the other eight parks, very little positive action was taken. A car park was constructed here and there, and a few uninspiring leaflets were produced, but apart from this these areas were little more than national parks in name only.

However, the pressure for change built up, and after further years of campaigning, important improvements to the system of national park administration were introduced in 1974, in conjunction with local government reorganisation. Although the government resisted the creation of more boards, it kept the two existing ones and set up new statutory national park committees for the other eight parks. These committees were set within the structure of the new county councils (for example, the Yorkshire Dales and North York Moors National Park committees are part of North Yorkshire County Council), but they had certain special features as well. One third of the members were to be appointed by the Secretary of State for the Environment. Approximately 75 per cent of the parks' funding was to come from central government. Each committee had to appoint a national park officer and supporting staff, and it also had to prepare a national park plan showing how it proposed to carry out its statutory duties in the various parts of the park.

At the time, the RA and other voluntary organisations regarded these measures as inadequate. They took the view that yet another opportunity had been wasted. However, while the superiority of boards over committees has remained apparent, the post-1974 system has proved to be a vast improvement on the old arrangements. In addition, more public funds have been directed to national parks, and a report by a committee chaired by Lord Sandford has led to a higher level of commitment to the objectives of national parks by county councils and some government departments. Tangible improvements since 1974 have been very noticeable. For example, walkers in national parks have seen many more signposts and waymarks on rights of way. Hundreds of new stiles and footbridges have been constructed; new trails for walkers of all abilities have been opened up; and there is an abundance of official literature on walks and footpaths in the parks.

So today, the boards versus committees argument is only of secondary importance. The issue at the fore is that of conflict between different government policies as they affect national parks, with particular reference to agricultural development.

The agricultural industry is heavily dependent upon government help in the form of grants, exemption from planning control and the price-support system. It follows that the government can exercise great influence over the nature and pace of agricultural change in a national park. But farming improvements can often harm the landscape and restrict public access. For example hill farmers on Exmoor (with strong support from the Ministry of Agriculture) have for many years been ploughing up moorland and turning it into enclosed pasture for intensive grazing. The open moor – the country that originally caused the area to be designated by ministers as a national park – has been disappearing at an alarming rate.

Only two simple measures are needed to stop this from happening. The first is for the Ministry of Agriculture to change its grant-making policies so that it only gives subsidies for operations that aid the conservation of the park's natural beauty. The second is for the national park committee to be empowered to make moorland conservation orders to prevent the loss of open country. These two issues were debated at length during the passage of the Wildlife and Countryside Bill through Parliament in 1981. The Ministry of Agriculture successfully resisted the introduction of these measures. Instead, much weaker provisions were put into the Bill. One required agricultural ministers to take account of conservation interests before awarding grants; another required farmers to give notice of their intention to plough moorland in limited areas.

Critics of the Wildlife and Countryside Act argue that it dodged the central issue of the need for *integrated* public policies on national parks. This theme is developed brilliantly and at length in a recent book by Ann and Malcolm MacEwen – a work called *National Parks – Conservation or Cosmetics?* (Allen and Unwin, published in January 1982). They demonstrate that current policies on grant-aid for agriculture and industry in national parks are not only harmful to conservation interests, but are also inimical to the long-term social and economic well-being of the local community. This is because current policies are biassed towards support for large, capital-intensive developments. Smaller, labour-intensive schemes (which by and large do not harm the landscape or wildlife and which provide more employment) receive much less assistance from government sources. While the Development Commission struggles to find a few thousand pounds to support light industries in rural areas, the Ministry of Agriculture, the Department of Industry and various nationalised industries lay out millions of pounds on schemes that usually damage the national park without bringing more than a handful of new permanent jobs to the area.

Research carried out by the MacEwens shows that this imbalance is also reflected in the membership of national park committees and boards. They found that a 'typical' member was an elderly male landowner of comfortable means. Those groups who are hardly represented at all are the recreational users of the national parks and local people who happen to be women, or working-class, or unemployed.

The MacEwens argue, as Colin Speakman has done, that there are many ways of using public funds that both achieve the objectives of the national park designation and that aid the local community living there. For example, instead of paying farmers to produce yet more milk and beef to add to the Common Market surpluses, the Ministry of Agriculture should use its funds to support traditional methods of farm management that both require more labour and conserve moorland, woodland, wetlands, hedgerows and other landscape features. Of course, this is not to say that farmers and agricultural workers should be driven back to the poverty line. Government subsidies should be directed towards ensuring that those who work on the land in national parks receive a good income in return for managing the countryside in the interests of conservation and public access. This need not lead to more public expenditure – simply a change in the way that it is allocated. The same policies can be applied to other areas, for example transport. Here again, the joint objectives should be to protect the environment, help people enjoy the national park and support the local community. These aims can be met by giving high priority to public transport, coupled with stricter traffic control (particularly of heavy through traffic and peak visitor traffic). Public transport minimises the impact of traffic on the countryside, helps visitors get about the national park (and frees walkers from having to plan circular walks all the time), and aids local communities. Some schemes – notably Dales Rail, the Goyt valley traffic management scheme, and the mini-bus services in the Lake District, Northumberland, Dartmoor and elsewhere – have already been implemented and have shown the way ahead. For more information about the successful operation of the Dales Rail service, see *Report of an experimental project in the Yorkshire Dales National Park* (Countryside Commission 1980). But much more can and should be done, even if we can never get to the ideal state of banning all cars from national parks and providing electric trains and buses to get people around!

The promotion of tourism in national parks also calls for reappraisal. It is notable that, in a number of places on the Continent, particularly in the alpine regions of Austria and Switzerland, all the paths are carefully waymarked, information boards giving the time and distance to various summits abound, and there is a feeling that, with due respect for privacy and property, one is welcome to walk almost anywhere. If only it were possible to say the same about national parks in this country!

Of course, tourism can be harmful to the environment. The MacEwens distinguish between two types of tourism – 'benign' and 'cataclysmic'. The 'benign' development of tourism places emphasis on expanding bed and breakfast accommodation in farmhouses and private dwellings; it encompasses the conversion of disused barns into simple youth hostels, as is now being pioneered in the Yorkshire Dales; and it bases itself upon the promotion of informal recreations like walking. 'Cataclysmic' tourism is the kind that leads to the construction of huge hotels and 'leisure complexes' promoting expensive and often noisy pastimes such as water-skiing. The buildings and associated works are intrusive, and the profits from such ventures are usually channelled away from the locality into the bank accounts of the big multi-national companies that run them. Needless to say, 'cataclysmic' tourism in national parks should be opposed with as much vigour as 'benign' tourism should be promoted.

Central to the success of the right kind of tourism in national parks is the provision of facilities for walking, which is by far the most popular outdoor recreation in this country. It was remarked earlier that important advances have been made in this area since 1974, but there is still a lot more to be done. For example, it is now thirty-two years since the National Parks and Access to the Countryside Act was placed on the statute-book. Yet there are still many areas of mountain, moor and heath in national parks to which the public has no or only limited access. This applies to the Aran mountains in Snowdonia, the defence lands of Pembrokeshire, Northumberland and Dartmoor, some of the shooting moors on the eastern heights of the Peak District, and so on. We should follow the example of some of our European neighbours and insist on a right of access on foot to all open country in national parks. Limited restrictions could be applied to allow grouse shooting to take place safely and any unavoidable military activities to be carried out. Some areas (preferably relatively small) could be set aside as nature reserves. Owners should be able to claim compensation from public funds if they incur damage that is attributable to the lifting of restrictions on access. To minimise such damage, bye-laws and warden services should be provided (much as they are now, but over a wider area).

Open country in national parks should be managed in the interests of conservation and public access. The National Trust, with its extensive hill estates in the Lake District and elsewhere, has demonstrated that this can be done successfully. These open areas should be regarded by all public and private bodies as part of our national heritage, and people

164

should be encouraged to visit, respect and cherish them. There should also be a review, carried out by the national park authorities, of facilities for public access on foot to areas of woodland and parkland and to shorelines, riverbanks and clifftops. Such areas are natural zones for walking. The growth in the popularity of walking has been particularly noticeable in the case of family parties taking relatively short walks in low-lying and coastal areas. The provision of more access to the type of country referred to above would therefore help meet this demand. The national park authorities have powers to make access orders and path creation orders (with compensation payable in both cases), and they should make much greater use of these powers than they have done to date.

And, finally, the highest possible priority should be given to maintaining rights of way in national parks. The construction and maintenance of costly information and visitor centres is all very laudable, but visitors might be better served if some national park authorities spent less on stuffed sheep and audio-visual displays, and more on putting up stiles, footbridges and waymarks.

The preparation and regular review of national park plans for walkers has been advocated by the MacEwens. One hesitates to support this, knowing that some national park authorities have used other official plans in the past as vehicles for promoting policies on footpath 'rationalisation' for example, see the reference to such plans in the chapter on the Pembrokeshire Coast National Park. Nevertheless, there is much to be said for establishing a means by which the authorities are obliged to think regularly and positively above the importance of walking as a recreation in national parks.

Of course, none of this will come about overnight. But it may never come about at all in some parks if the boards and committees are not subject to continual public pressure. I therefore hope that it is not too out of place to end this chapter with a small plug for the two organisations working in this field with which I am most closely connected.

The Ramblers' Association was established as a national organisation under that title in 1935 and has worked tirelessly over the years in the interests of national parks and the folk who enjoy exploring them on foot. It has over 37,000 members and is aiming for 50,000 by the time of its fiftieth anniversary in 1985. It played a very active part in influencing the form that legislation affecting national parks and rights of way took in 1949, 1968 and 1981. It has over 200 local groups throughout the country and membership of a local group is free to anyone paying an RA subscription. Its address is 1/5 Wandsworth Road, London SW8 2LJ.

The Council for National Parks is an 'umbrella' organisation – one that has as members nearly forty national and regional voluntary organisations concerned about conservation or recreation in national parks. It was established in 1936 as the Standing Committee on National Parks, initially with the objective of having national parks designated, and subsequently with the aim of keeping a careful watch on developments in the parks, and of making appropriate representations when a park seemed threatened in any way. It does not have individual members as such, but there is a scheme for 'Friends of National Parks' under which, in return for a regular donation, a card and a newsletter are dispatched. The council's address is 4 Hobart Place, London SW1W 0HY.

The fact that we have national parks at all is in no small measure due to the work of these two organisations. If you believe that their work is worth supporting, then write to them for further information before you finally lay down this book, pack your rucksack and head for the hills.

Appendix

The national parks – basic data

	Date of designation	Area (sq miles)	Highest point
Dartmoor	1951	365	2,040ft, 622m (High Willhays)
Exmoor	1954	265	1,700ft, 518m (Dunkery Beacon)
Peak District	1951	542	2,084ft, 635m (Kinder Scout)
Yorkshire Dales	1954	680	2,419ft, 737m (Whernside)
North York Moors	1952	553	1,490ft, 454m (Urra Moor)
Northumberland	1956	398	2,674ft, 815m (The Cheviot)
Lake District	1951	866	3,206ft, 977m (Scafell Pikes)
Brecon Beacons	1957	519	2,907ft, 886m (Pen y Fan)
Pembrokeshire Coast	1952	225	1,760ft, 537m (Foel Cwmcerwyn)
Snowdonia	1951	840	3,560ft, 1,085m (Snowdon)

The National Park Offices

(Addresses for correspondence only)

Dartmoor – 'Parke', Haytor Road, Bovey Tracey, Devon

Exmoor – Exmoor House, Dulverton, Somerset

Peak District – National Park Office, Baslow Road, Bakewell, Derbyshire

Yorkshire Dales – 'Colvend', Hebden Road, Grassington, N Yorks

North York Moors – The Old Vicarage, Bondgate, Helmsley, N Yorks

Northumberland – Eastburn, South Park, Hexham, Northumberland

Lake District – National Park Office, Busher Walk, Kendal, Cumbria

Brecon Beacons – National Park Office, Glamorgan St, Brecon, Powys

Pembrokeshire Coast – County Offices, Haverfordwest, Dyfed

Snowdonia – Yr Hen Ysgol, Maentwrog, Gwynedd

National park information centres

Note: Most centres are open only during the summer months (normally Easter to October). A few are open only at weekends. Some information centres are located in mobile caravans which may not always be in the position indicated.

Dartmoor	Newbridge	SX 711709
	Postbridge	SX 647789
	Steps Bridge	SX 803883
	Tavistock	SX 482745
Exmoor	Combe Martin	SS 576474
	County Gate	SS 793487
	Lynmouth	SS 724494
	Minehead	SS 968462
Peak District	Bakewell (Market Hall)	SK 217685
	Castleton	SK 150828
	Dovestones	SE 013034
	Edale	SK 124856
	Goyt Valley	SK 018716
	Hartington	SK 149611
	Tideswell Dale	SK 154742
Yorkshire Dales	Aysgarth Falls	SE 012888
	Clapham	SD 745693
	Hawes	SD 876899
	Malham	SD 901628
	Sedbergh	SD 658922
North York Moors	Danby Lodge	NZ 716084
	Pickering	SE 797842
	Sutton Bank	SE 515831
Northumberland	Byrness	NT 765028
	Harbottle Hills	NT 927048
	Ingram	NU 020163
	Once Brewed	NY 753669
	Rothbury	NU 057016
Lake District	Ambleside	NY 375045
	Bowness	SD 400966
	Brockhole	NY 389010

	Coniston	SD 303976
	Glenridding	NY 386171
	Hawkshead	SD 354981
	Keswick	NY 266234
	Pooley Bridge	NY 471243
	Seatoller	SD 245137
	Waterhead	NY 377033
Brecon Beacons	Abergavenny	SO 301142
	Brecon	SO 045284
	Llandovery	SN 768343
	Mountain Centre	SN 977262
Pembrokeshire Coast	Broad Haven	SM 863141
	Fishguard	SM 958370
	Haverfordwest	SM 954156
	Kilgetty	SN 122072
	Pembroke	SM 983016
	St David's	SM 754253
	Tenby	SN 133008
Snowdonia	Aberdyfi	SN 614959
	Bala	SH 927361
	Blaenau Ffestiniog	SH 698459
	Conwy	SH 783777
	Dolgellau	SH 729179
	Harlech	SH 579313
	Llanberis	SH 583596
	Llanwrst	SH 799615
	Plas Tan-y-bwlch	SH 655403

Accommodation

For information about hotels, guest houses and farmhouse accommodation in national parks, contact the local offices of the regional tourist boards. They usually offer a booking service. The head offices of the tourist boards are:

English Tourist Board – 4 Grosvenor Gardens, London SW1 0DU.
Wales Tourist Board – 2 Fitzalan Road, Cardiff CF2 1UY

The Ramblers' Association publishes an annual *Bed and Breakfast Guide* which lists moderately priced establishments that are happy to welcome ramblers. Some other publications giving details of accommodation are also available from the RA. Send an sae and ask for a sales item list. The RA's address is:

1/5 Wandsworth Road, London SW8 2LJ.

The Youth Hostels Association has a considerable number of youth hostels in all the national parks. Prices for overnight accommodation are extremely reasonable, and membership is open to people of all ages. For further details write to the YHA at:

Trevelyan House, St Stephens Hill, St Albans, Herts AL1 2DY.

Ramblers' Association Services Ltd run a fine centre for walkers at Hassness, on the shores of Buttermere in the Lake District. You book for a week at a time and a leader takes parties on walks around the surrounding fells. For details write to RAS at:

13 Longcroft House, Fretherne Road, Welwyn Garden City, Herts.

The Countrywide Holidays Association and the Holiday Fellowship also run walkers' centres at a number of places throughout Britain, including locations in some of the national parks (eg, Whitby and Ambleside). For details write to:

CHA – Birch Heys, Cromwell Range, Manchester MI4 8HU.

HF – 142 Great North Way, Hendon, London NW4 1EG.

Campers can often obtain information on camping sites from national park information centres. In addition, the following organisations offer very helpful services:

Backpackers' Club – 20 St Michael's Road, Tilehurst, Reading, Berks RG3 4RP.

Camping Club – 11 Lower Grosvenor Place, London SW1W 0EY.

Finally, some of the national park offices now publish accommodation guides for their respective national park. Write to the addresses given above for details.

Maps, books and other publications

Note: No prices are quoted for the publications mentioned below because they change too quickly. However, those marked with an asterisk are relatively cheap booklets and paperbacks. A few of the publications (including all the OS maps) are on sale from the RA office. Please send a sae and ask for a sales item list. Others are often available in good bookshops in and around the national parks, and in national park information centres. In London, good stockists of maps and walks guides are:

Cook, Hammond and Kell Ltd, 22 Caxton St, SW1.

Stanfords Ltd, 12 Long Acre, WC2.

YHA Shop, 14 Southampton St, WC2.

General publications on walking and the national parks
Walking in the Countryside David Sharp in collaboration with the
   Ramblers' Association (David & Charles)
Walking Old Railways Christopher Somerville (David & Charles)
Britain's National Parks edited by Mervyn Bell (David & Charles)
Roads and Tracks of Britain Christopher Taylor (David & Charles)
The Outdoor Survival Handbook D. Platten (David & Charles)
The Big Walks compiled by Ken Wilson and Richard Gilbert
   (Diadem)
Walking Through Northern England Charlie Emett and Mike Hutton
   (David & Charles)
English Mountain Summits Nick Wright (Robert Hale)
First Aid for Hillwalkers and Climbers J. Renouf and S. Hulse
   (Penguin)
*Wales Walking** (Wales Tourist Board)
Walks in Wales Roger Jones (Robert Hale)
The Welsh Peaks W. A. Poucher (Constable)

In addition there is an HMSO official guide to each national park.

Magazines and newsletters with regular information and articles
about walking in national parks and other parts of the country
include:
Climber and Rambler (Holmes McDougall): the official journal of
   the British Mountaineering Council, with the emphasis more on
   mountaineering.
Hostelling News: the newsletter of the YHA.
Rucksack: the official journal of the Ramblers' Association, with
   regular news about maps, books and guides.
Strider: the official journal of the Long Distance Walkers' Association, with a full listing of forthcoming 'challenge walks'.
The Great Outdoors (Holmes McDougall): the monthly magazine for
   walkers and backpackers, with regular news about the RA and
   about equipment, publications and walking areas.

The Forestry Commission publishes a range of guides and leaflets
about trails on its estates. Useful maps for planning walks on forest
trails are:
*See Your Forests**: South England
                     North England
                     Wales

APPENDIX

The Long-distance paths

Several long-distance paths have been mentioned in the preceding chapters. Publications dealing with these are listed below.

GENERAL READING

Long Distance Paths in England and Wales T. G. Miller (David & Charles)

Ramblers' Ways edited by David Sharp (David & Charles). An introduction to some of the 'unofficial' long-distance walks of England and Wales. Available from RA national office.

The Long Distance Walker's Handbook Alan and Barbara Blatchford (Long Distance Walkers Association). A guide to long-distance routes and challenge walks.

Long Distance Path Wall Chart* (*The Great Outdoors*). Includes 90 paths.

Across Northern Hills Geoffrey Berry (*Westmorland Gazette*). Describes 9 long-distance paths walks in northern England.

Long Distance Footpaths and Bridleways (by and from Countryside Commission). Free general leaflet about 'official' paths.

CLEVELAND WAY

93-mile horseshoe-shaped route around the North York Moors providing in equal measure moorland (Helmsley to Saltburn) and coastal scenery (Saltburn to Filey). Maps: OS 1:50,000 sheets 93, 94, 99, 100, 101.

The Cleveland Way (Countryside Commission leaflet)

The Cleveland Way Alan Falconer (HMSO)

A Guide to the Cleveland Way Malcolm Boyes (Constable). Includes details of a link from Scarborough to Helmsley.

Cleveland Way Information (from North York Moors National Park Office).

The Cleveland Way* W. Cowley (Dalesman)

COAST TO COAST WALK

190 miles from St Bees to Robin Hood's Bay (Whitby) through three national parks: Lake District, Yorkshire Dales, North York Moors. Maps: OS 1:50,000 sheets 89, 90, 91, 92, 93, 94, 98, 99.

A Coast to Coast Walk. A Wainwright (*Westmorland Gazette*)

CUMBRIA WAY

70 miles from Ulverston in the south to Carlisle in the north. Maps: OS 1:50,000 sheets 85, 90, 97.

Cumbria Way* John Trevelyan (Dalesman)

172

DALES WAY

81-mile riverside route from Ilkley in West Yorkshire to Bowness (Windermere) in Cumbria. Waymarked in part. Maps: OS 1:50,000 sheets 97, 98, 104.
*Dales Way** Colin Speakman (Dalesman)
*Dales Way Handbook** (by and from RA West Riding Area). Also from RA national office.

DERBYSHIRE GRITSTONE WAY

56 miles from Derby to Edale following the gritstone edges and moors of north Derbyshire. Maps: OS 1:50,000 sheets 119, 128; OS 1in Tourist Map of Peak District (northern section); OS 1:25,000 Outdoor Leisure Map of the White Peak (southern section).
*The Derbyshire Gritstone Way** Steve Burton, Max Maughan and Ian Quarrington (Thornhill Press)

DERWENT WAY

80 miles following the River Derwent from Barmby-on-the-Marsh (Goole) to Lilla Howe on the North York Moors. Maps: OS 1:50,000 sheets 100, 101, 106.
*The Derwent Way** Richard C. Kenchington (Dalesman)

HADRIAN'S WALL

The Wall extends for 73 miles from Wallsend near Newcastle to Bowness on the Solway Firth. Only about 10 miles of the Wall are extant, though earthwork evidence makes it possible to trace the route for many more miles. Continuity is disrupted by roads laid over the Wall and by an absence of rights of way in places. The finest open and unspoilt section is a 15-mile stretch from Sewingshields Crags to Walltown Crags, which is followed in part by the Pennine Way. Maps: OS 1:50,000 sheets 85, 86, 87, 88; OS 2in Hadrian's Wall Map (this does not show public rights of way).
A Walk Along the Wall Hunter Davies (Weidenfeld & Nicholson)
*Guide to Walking Hadrian's Wall** Graham Mizon (Hendon Publishing Co, Ltd)
*A Guide to Hadrian's Wall** A. R. Birley (HMSO)
*Rambling along the Roman Wall** (RA Northern Area)
Roman Wall summer bus service (free details from Northumberland National Park Office)

OFFA'S DYKE PATH

168 miles along the Welsh border from Chepstow and the Severn estuary to Prestatyn on Liverpool Bay. For some 60 miles the path

runs along or is close to the earthwork constructed in the eighth century by Offa, King of Mercia, to denote his boundary with the Welsh. The route is fully signposted and waymarked in part, but use of a compass may be necessary over the occasional moorland stretch. The Offa's Dyke Association exists to promote and protect the path. Members receive newsletters and up-to-date 'state of the path' information. Details from ODA c/o the Correspondence Secretary, Old Primary School, Knighton, Powys. Maps: OS 1:50,000 sheets 116, 117, 126, 137, 148, 161, 162. (See also strip maps below.)

*Strip maps of the Offa's Dyke Path** Tony Drake and Allan Russell (ODA). Nine double-sided sheets of two-colour reproductions from OS 1:25,000 maps; complete set with key map.

*Path Guide Notes** (ODA)
  (a) North–South
  (b) South–North (greater detail)
  Designed to accompany the strip maps.

Through Welsh Border Country following Offa's Dyke Path Mark Richards (Thornhill Press)

A Guide to Offa's Dyke Path C. J. Wright (Constable)

Offa's Dyke Path John B. Jones (HMSO)

*Offa's Dyke Path Accommodation and Transport List** (by and from ODA). Also from RA national office.

PEAKLAND WAY

96-mile circular walk around the Peak District National Park. Maps: OS 1:50,000 sheets 110, 119; Peak District 1in Tourist Map.

*Peakland Way** John Merrill (Dalesman)

PEMBROKESHIRE COAST PATH

168 miles following the coastline of Pembrokeshire from Amroth to Cardigan. Extensively signed and waymarked, but walking the route is often strenuous. Maps: OS 1:50,000 sheets 145, 157, 158.

Pembrokeshire Coast Path (Countryside Commission leaflet)

Pembrokeshire Coast Path John Barrett (HMSO)

*Walking the Pembrokeshire Coast Path** Patrick Stark (H. G. Walters Ltd, Tenby). With accommodation list.

PENNINE WAY

First of the official long-distance paths to be established, it still remains the most challenging. From Edale in the Peak District to Kirk Yetholm over the Scottish border, the Way traverses the high moorland of the Pennine Hills for 250 miles. It is signposted and cairned where necessary, nevertheless the ability to use a compass is essential. The Pennine Way Council exists to protect and promote the route. Details of membership from the Hon Treasurer, 14 St Barnabas Drive, Littleborough, Lancs OL15 8EJ. Maps: OS 1:50,000 sheets 74, 80, 86, 91, 92, 98, 103, 109, 110.

Pennine Way (Countryside Commission leaflet)
Pennine Way* Tom Stephenson (RA national office)
Pennine Way Tom Stephenson (HMSO)
Pennine Way Companion A. Wainwright (*Westmorland Gazette*)
A Guide to the Pennine Way C. J. Wright (3rd edition, Constable)
Pennine Way Accommodation List* Pennine Way Council (from John Needham or RA national office)
Pennine Way Pub Guide* John Jowett, Rob Mellor and Paul Wilson (from Paul Wilson)

SOUTH WEST PENINSULA COAST PATH (SOUTH WEST WAY)
Total mileage varies from 515 (Countryside Commission) to 546 (SW Way Association). Either way, this route is by far the longest in Britain, running from Minehead in Somerset down to Land's End, and thence along the southern coast to South Haven Point in Poole Harbour, Dorset. The South West Way Association has as its aim 'the satisfactory completion of the Path as a continuous coastal route'. Members receive newsletters with up-to-date 'state of the path' information and footpath descriptions. Details of membership can be obtained from Mary Macleod, 1 Orchard Drive, Kingskerswell, Devon TQ12 5DG. The association publishes a most useful annual *Complete Guide to the Coastal Path** (new editions normally published in January) giving accommodation, bibliography, transport and 'state of the path' information. Maps (Somerset and North Devon section – 82 miles, Minehead to near Bude): OS 1:50,000 sheets 180, 181, 190.

Exmoor National Park* (South West Way Association)
  Minehead to Lynmouth; Lynmouth to Combe Martin (footpath descriptions)
Somerset and North Devon; Cornwall; South Devon and Dorset (Countryside Commission leaflets)
Somerset and North Devon Coast Path: Exmoor Section* (Exmoor National Park Office)
Coast link (bus service details free from Exmoor National Park Office)
Minehead to St Ives Ken Ward and John Mason (Letts)

TWO MOORS WAY

103 miles from Ivybridge in South Devon to Lynton on the North Devon Coast crossing Dartmoor and Exmoor. Use of a compass may be necessary across the moors. The route is waymarked across mid-Devon. Maps: OS 1:50,000 sheets 202, 191, 181, 180; OS 1in Tourist Maps of Dartmoor and Exmoor.

*Two Moors Way** (RA Devon Area). Also from RA national office.

Ordnance Survey maps

There is a nationwide coverage of 1:50,000 OS maps, nearly all of which show rights of way. The Second Series 1:25,000 (Pathfinder) maps cover only part of the country, although more maps are being published all the time. However, at the time of writing, only northern Dartmoor and the southern part of the Peak District are reasonably well covered by this series. Fortunately, most national parks are covered by a special Tourist or Outdoor Leisure map. Details are as follows:

	1:50,000 maps	*Other OS maps*
Dartmoor	191, 201, 202	1in Tourist Map
Exmoor	180, 181	1in Tourist Map
Peak District	109, 110, 118, 119	1in Tourist Map
		Outdoor Leisure 1:25,000 Maps of The White Peak and the Dark Peak
Yorkshire Dales	92, 97, 98, 99, 103, 104	1:25,000 Outdoor Leisure Maps of Malham and Upper Wharfedale, and The Three Peaks
North York moors	93, 94, 99, 100, 101	1in Tourist Map
Northumberland	74, 75, 80, 81, 86, 87	1:31,680 strip map of Hadrian's Wall
Lake District	85, 89, 90, 96, 97	1:25,000 Outdoor Leisure Maps (four separate sheets) 1in Tourist Map.
Brecon Beacons	146, 159, 160, 161, 171	1:25,000 Outdoor Leisure Maps (three separate sheets)
Pembrokeshire Coast	145, 157, 158	The HMSO guide to the coast path contains 1:25,000 maps for the whole route.
Snowdonia	115, 116, 124, 125, 135	1:25,000 Outdoor Leisure Maps (five separate sheets). ½in Tourist Map

For a free catalogue of OS maps write to the OS at Romsey Road, Maybush, Southampton SO9 4DH.

APPENDIX

Guides listed by National Park

It is always advisable to write to the national park office in advance of a visit and ask for a publications' list. Most of the park offices keep a very comprehensive range of publications in stock, including a large number of their own leaflets and booklets describing walks in their parks.

DARTMOOR

The Dartmoor Preservation Association publishes a bibliography of Dartmoor, and this provides a full list of background references. Still the best single publication – the 'classic of Dartmoor literature' – is *Crossing's Guide to Dartmoor*, first published in 1909 and reprinted in 1966 with a new introduction by Brian Le Messurier, which outlines the most significant changes on the moor since the guide first appeared. It was written primarily for walkers and it describes in minute detail dozens of walking 'excursions' on the moor. It has a fascinating section entitled 'Packhorse tracks and other old paths' which is not only a useful guide to route planning, but also an absorbing insight into the history of Dartmoor. The enduring value of *Crossing's Guide* highlights the man's simple modesty. He concluded the preface to the first edition with the words:

> If I gain the confidence of the rambler who uses this book my satisfaction will be complete. There is some reason for me to hope that I shall do so, as I venture to believe that he will discover ere we have gone far on our wanderings together that I am really and truly a Dartmoor man.

Crossing's work has been supplemented by many more recent walking guides. Brian Le Messurier has himself produced a book in the Frederick Warne series of short circular walks for motorists. The Dartmoor National Park Committee has published some walking guides and there is also Hugh Westacott's *Walks and Rides on Dartmoor*. These latter guides describe what are mostly short walks (less than 10 miles).

Dartmoor by Crispin Gill (David & Charles)
Crossing's Guide to Dartmoor (David & Charles)
*Bus away Walk-a-day** V. Wilson and P. Martin (Dartmoor National Park Office)
*Walks in the Dartmoor National Park** (Dartmoor National Park Office)
No 1 Moretonhampstead, Manaton and Lustleigh
No 2 South West
No 3 Postbridge to Ashburton

177

The Dartmoor Bibliography* (Dartmoor Preservation Association)
Visitors' Guides* Arthur L. Clamp (Westway Publications, 203
Elburton Road, Plymouth, Devon PL9 8HX)
Eastern Dartmoor; Northern Dartmoor; Southern Dartmoor;
Exeter; Plymouth;
South Hams; Torbay. (Each contains 11 walks.)
Walks and Rides on Dartmoor* H. D. Westacott (Footpath Publica-
tions, Adstock Cottage, Adstock, Buckingham MK18 2HZ)
Walks for Motorists (Frederick Warne)
– *Dartmoor** Brian Le Messurier
– *South Devon* Alan Coles
Eight Walks from Bovey Tracey* E. R. Vinnicombe (Mr E. R. Vinni-
combe, Beechcroft, Coombe Cross, Bovey Tracey, Newton
Abbot, Devon)

EXMOOR

An excellent guide to the Exmoor section of the South West Way is
published by the national park office and this is best supplemented by
the South West Way Association's annual *Complete Guide to the
Coastal Path*. This gives a tremendous amount of information on
accommodation, camp sites, bus services and the state of the path.
The association has battled for a better path since it was formed in
1973, and the *Guide* contains some apt and occasionally acid
comments about the failure of authority to have the path shifted off
metalled roads at a number of points.

The wildlife, legends and history of Exmoor have inspired many
writers and there is much excellent literature on the national park.
The park office produces a list of publications – all of which it sells –
which includes general tourist guides and publications produced by
Exmoor Press. The latter are inexpensive and very informative.
Exmoor Press also publishes the annual journal *Exmoor Review*,
which is the journal of the Exmoor Society. It is usually full of fascinating stories and articles about the life and landscape of Exmoor. The
1in Tourist Map is invaluable in depicting public rights of way,
major viewpoints, National Trust land and other features.

The Exmoor National Park Committee publishes a number of
booklets describing the short 'Waymarked Walks'. These contain
excellent 1:25,000 maps. The park office also publishes booklets
describing nature trails on North Hill and at Cloutsham (in the
woods to the north of Dunkery Hill). Short walks in Exmoor are also
described in booklets published by Spurbooks and Frederick Warne.

APPENDIX

Exmoor National Park Authority publications*:
Cloutsham Nature Trail
North Hill Nature Trail
Short Walks from County Gate
Suggested Walks and Bridleways: North Devon (Combe Martin, Woody Bay, Lynton/Lynmouth, Malmsmead, Brendon Common)
Walks on North Hill, Minehead
Waymarked Walks 1 (Dunster, Minehead, Brendon Hill, Luxborough, Roadwater)
Waymarked Walks 2 (Porlock, Oare, Dunkery, Malmsmead, Exford, Simonsbath)
Waymarked Walks 3 (Dulverton, Winsford Hill, Tarr Steps, Anstey Common, Haddeo Valley)
Rambles in West Somerset and on Exmoor (free from Western National Omnibus Co Ltd, National House, Queen Street, Exeter, Devon EX4 3TF)
*Walks for Motorists – Exmoor** David Butler (Frederick Warne)
Exmoor Coastal Walks; Exmoor Riverside Walks*; Exmoor Walks** all by Tim Abbott (Books of Wessex Ltd) Priory Bridge Road, Taunton, Somerset)

THE PEAK DISTRICT

The histories of the old drove roads and green lanes have been described in great detail by A. & E. Dodd in their book *Peakland Roads and Trackways*, and a study of this volume can greatly enrich a day's walk along tracks and paths in the peak.

First and Last (Peak Park Planning Board)
Freedom to Roam Howard Hill (Moorland)
Peakland Roads and Trackways A. E. and E. M. Dodd (Moorland)
Derbyshire: Exploring the Ancient Tracks S. Toulson (Wildwood House)
*Walks in the Peak District** Lindsey Porter (Spurbooks)
*Peak District Walks** John Merrill (Dalesman)
– *1 Short Walks*
– *2 Long Walks*
*Derbyshire Trails** John Merrill (Dalesman)
*Walking in South Derbyshire** John Merrill (Dalesman)
Walks for Motorists C. Thompson (Frederick Warne)
– *Derbyshire, Northern Area**
– *Peak District**

179

APPENDIX

Peak Park Joint Planning Board publications (National Park Office):
Access Map* (2½in to the mile): Eastern Edges and Stanage Edge
Access Map* (1in to the mile): Kinder, Bleaklow, Longdendale,
Langsett and Chew Moors
Goyt Valley Booklet*
Tissington and High Peak Trails*
Walks Around*: *Bakewell*
Dovedale
Edale
Eyam and Hathersage
Hartington and Railway Trails
Longdendale
White Peak – Short Walks*
White Peak – Walks linking Youth Hostels*
Walks from your Car – East Cheshire* Barbara Brill (Dalesman).
Macclesfield-Buxton area; short strolls.
Pathwise in Glossop and Longdendale (by and from David Frith)
Six Walks around Whaley Bridge* (by and from the RA New Mills
and District Group) Short walks.

THE YORKSHIRE DALES

A booklet about the Reginald Farrer Trail is available from national park centres, and the national park office has also produced an impressive number of other leaflets and guides to waymarked walks in the Dales. The leaflets are excellent, giving OS maps, clear directions, advice on terrain, parking and public transport and information on points of interest along the walk.

As well as the official national park walks leaflets, there are many other publications describing paths and walks in the Yorkshire Dales. Pre-eminent among these – and setting a national standard – are the footpath maps and guides produced by Arthur Gemmell. The maps are drawn on a scale of 2½in to the mile and show in meticulous detail the location of rights of way in relation to roads, villages, rivers and major topographical features. The amount of detail is remarkable – for instance, individual stiles are shown, and indications are given of the state of the path (eg, muddy in winter). They are accompanied by notes with details of suggested walks. At the time of writing, the maps cover the Three Peaks area and the country around Bolton Abbey, Aysgarth, Grassington, Sedbergh, Malham and Hawes.

Dalesman have – not surprisingly – published a number of walking guides for the national park. The descriptions are accompanied by sketch maps only, so the walker must take an OS map with him when using one of these books. But they have been written by people who know their country well – Colin Speakman has one on the Craven

180

Dales (that is the dales in the southern and western sections of the park) Geoffrey White has written books on Wensleydale and Swaledale; and the RA North Yorks and South Durham Area has compiled a book in the same series on walking in the northern dales. Dalesman also publish a booklet which describes the route of the Three Peaks Walk and relates much of the history of the surrounding area. The West Riding Area of the Ramblers' Association has compiled three books in the Frederick Warne series of rambles for motorists. For general guides to the Yorkshire Dales, Arthur Raistrick's HMSO guide is clearly the most authoritative and contains an excellent bibliography. Dalesman also produce their own *Guide to the Yorkshire Dales*, which describes each of the major dales in turn and is well illustrated. From all this it must be clear that the Yorkshire Dales is a very popular area for walking – certainly the public demand for literature about walks and footpaths seems insatiable.

The Dalesman Guide to the Yorkshire Dales* (Dalesman)
Yorkshire's Three Peaks* (Dalesman)
Walking in the Craven Dales* Colin Speakman (Dalesman)
Walking in Upper Wharfedale* Mike Obst (Dalesman)
Walks in the Northern Dales compiled by the RA North Yorks and
    South Durham Area (Dalesman)
Walks in Wensleydale* Geoffrey White (Dalesman)
Walks in Swaledale* Geoffrey White (Dalesman)
Arthur Gemmell's Footpath Maps* (Stile Publications, Otley):
    Parklink Walks in Upper Wharfedale (A booklet of walks)
    Grassington and District
    Three Peaks
    Malhamdale
    Bolton Abbey
    Sedbergh
Walks in the Yorkshire Dales* H. O. Wade (Spurbooks)
Rambles in the Dales* Compiled by the RA West Riding Area (Fre-
    derick Warne)
Yorkshire Dales Walks for Motorists* compiled by the RA West
    Riding Area (Frederick Warne)
Further Dales Walks for Motorists* compiled by the RA West Riding
    Area (Frederick Warne)

THE NORTH YORK MOORS

For general guides to the park, Arthur Raistrick's HMSO guide and Harry Mead's less comprehensive but more evocative book *Inside the North York Moors* offer excellent reading. As for local walks guides, there is plenty of choice. At the time of writing, Frederick Warne have two books by Geoffrey White in their series of walks for motorists, there being thirty walks of 10 miles or under in each one. There are also several guides in the Dalesman's mini-book series. Some of these have been produced by the North Yorks and South Durham Area of the Ramblers' Association and are to be recommended for that reason alone! Like the Frederick Warne books, they describe walks of under 10 miles and are mainly written for motorists. However, some of them do give useful information about public transport as well.

A famous little guide that walkers in the area would do well to consult is *Horne's Guide to Whitby and District* (Seventy-Seventh edition). Although its suggestions for walks lack the maps and detailed step-by-step descriptions that walkers have rightly come to expect from their guides, *Horne's guide* captures the charm and antiquity of the area so well that such shortcomings are forgiven.

The national park office produces an impressive list of 'Waymark' and other leaflets and guides describing short walks and special trails, and – once again – the 1in Ordnance Survey Tourist Map of the area is an invaluable source of information and shows the open country and rights of way.

The descriptions and accompanying notes in Geoffrey White's book of walks for motorists are very good indeed.

Several of the walk guides for this part offer suggestions for circular walks based on the disused Scarborough – Whitby – Loftus railway track.

Inside the North York Moors Harry Mead (David & Charles)
A Visitor's Handbook to the North York Moors (National Park Office)
North York Moors Walks for Motorists* Geoffrey White (Frederick Warne)
  – *West and South*
  – *North and East*
Walking on the North York Moors* RA North Yorks and South Durham Area (Dalesman)
Walks from your Car* (Dalesman)
  – *Bilsdale and the Hambletons* RA
  – *Rosedale and Farndale* Malcolm Boyes
  – *Eskdale and the Cleveland Coast* RA
Horne's Guide to Whitby and District* (Horne & Son, Whitby)
The Derwent Way* Richard Kenchington (Dalesman)
The Lyke Wake Walk* Bill Cowley (Dalesman)
The White Rose Walk* Geoffrey White (Dalesman)
The Bilsdale Circuit* Michael Teanby (Dalesman)

NORTHUMBERLAND

The special trails in the park have been listed in a useful little publication, *Walks and Trails in Northumbria*, published by the Northumbria Tourist Board. This guide gives for each walk details of access by car and public transport, the distance and nature of the walk, and the place from which a leaflet or further information can be obtained.

The Northern Area of the Ramblers' Association have produced a booklet, *Ramblers through Northumberland*, which includes descriptions of a number of walks on the outskirts of the national park. The walks are clearly described and admirably illustrated.

Walks and Trails in Northumbria (Northumbria Tourist Board)
Ramblers' Tynedale (RA Northern Area)
Ramblers through Northumberland (RA Northern Area)
Walks for Motorists: Northumberland compiled by members of the RA Northern Area (Frederick Warne)

THE LAKE DISTRICT

There is literature in profusion for the walker seeking information about the Lake District. The national park office has produced a small (10p) leaflet that lists a host of books, maps and leaflets about the area. The office also produces some helpful leaflets on short walks in the park. If your funds are limited make sure that you first buy a set of OS Outdoor Leisure Maps (at a scale of 1:25,000), because the information packed into these is more comprehensive and more accurate than that contained in any guide-book. The 1in OS Tourist Map conveniently covers the whole national park and is an excellent map in its own right. But for serious fell walking, use the 1in for planning walks and the 1:25,000 maps for actual navigation on the tops.

Unique to the Lake District is that elegant, handy and often very amusing series of guides to the fells produced by Wainwright and entitled *A Pictorial Guide to the Lakeland Fells*. The seven books in this series have since been supplemented by a number of other publications by Wainwright – notably his book on the outlying fells of Lakeland, which has a particularly good coverage of the fells in the lower-lying southern and south-eastern sectors of the national park. These guides have attained a high reputation and many regular fell walkers find them invaluable.

The Wainwright guides are for those who want to get on to the ridges and summits. For walks lower down, there are many other guides, usually obtainable in bookshops in the Lake District. Both

APPENDIX

Frederick Warne and Dalesman have a number of walks guides to the area. The Lake District Area of the Ramblers' Association also publishes guides to walks in various parts of the national park, mainly on the lower fells and around the lakes. The Area is also associated with the annual publication *The Lakeland Rambler*, which is worthy of note here because it contains a number of walk descriptions for visitors to the national park.

More general publications include the official HMSO guide to the national park. This is rather more useful to the walker than others in this series, because it actually contains some interesting suggestions for valley-and-ridge walks in the area. Spencer's guide, referred to below, also contains some ideas for (usually) short walks and is a well-illustrated mine of information that complements the Ordnance Survey maps very well. There are no end of other books on the Lake District, but one to be recommended with particular enthusiasm is *The Lake District: A Century of Conservation* by Geoffrey Berry and Geoffrey Beard. This tells the story of how the unmatchable natural beauty of Lakeland has been fought for and retained by the work of voluntary conservation organisations, planning authorities, land-owners and others over the years. It is liberally illustrated with photographs by Geoffrey Berry, whose ability to capture on film both the magical attraction of the Lake District and the grotesqueness of some of the scars that have been inflicted upon it has brought him national renown.

A leaflet produced by the national park office lists seventeen of the nature trails and forest trails, with the location of their starting points. Many of the trails are described briefly in a book by Brian Spencer – *A Visitor's Guide to the Lake District* – in which distances and opening times (where appropriate) are given. Inexpensive leaflets describing each walk are obtainable at the starting points of the walks and/or in information centres throughout the park.

A Pictorial Guide to the Lakeland Fells A. Wainwright (*Westmorland Gazette*)
    Book 1 *The Eastern Fells*
    Book 2 *The Far Eastern Fells*
    Book 3 *The Central Fells*
    Book 4 *The Southern Fells*
    Book 5 *The Northern Fells*
    Book 6 *The North Western Fells*
    Book 7 *The Western Fells*
Walks on the Howgill Fells A. Wainwright (*Westmorland Gazette*)
The Outlying Fells of the Lake District A. Wainwright (*Westmorland Gazette*)

A Visitor's Guide to the Lake District Brian Spencer (Moorland)

The Lake District: A Century of Conservation Geoffrey Berry and Geoffrey Beard (John Bartholomew)

Walking in Northern Lakeland* (Dalesman)

Lake District Walks for Motorists* 3 volumes, John Parker (Frederick Warne)

    Central Area (Grasmere, Ambleside, Windermere, Coniston)

    Northern Area (Keswick, Borrowdale, Ullswater)

    Western Area (Buttermere, Wastwater, Eskdale, Duddon Valley, East of Coniston and to the coast)

The Martindale Guide* (from The Martindale Vicarage, Howtown, Nr Pooley Bridge, or The Ullswater Navigation and Transit Company, 13 Maude Street, Kendal, Cumbria). Includes a guide to all public paths in the Parish of Martindale.

Scafell Pikes Panorama* Chris Jesty (Jesty's Panoramas, Sunlyn, Allington Park, Bridport, Dorset DT6 5DD)

A set of three guides compiled by the RA Lake District Area (available from 62 Loop Road North, Whitehaven, Cumbria)

THE BRECON BEACONS

The history of some of the old cattle routes is told in the superbly illustrated *The Drovers' Roads of Wales* by Fay Godwin and Shirley Toulson.

The park authority publishes a number of leaflets describing mainly short walks from various centres, such as Brecon and Abergavenny. (One of these leaflets gives some short walks in Govilon, taking in part of the railway line and lengths of the canal). There are dozens of suggestions for walks in the park in the Wales Tourist Board's *Wales Walking* booklet.

Exploring the Brecon Beacons National Park Chris Barber (Regional Publications, 5 Springfield Road, Abergavenny, Gwent NP7 5TD)

Tracking through Mercia, Volume 2 Donna Baker (Express Logic Ltd, Hereford). 24 walks, 6 of them in the Black Mountains.

The Drovers' Roads of Wales Fay Godwin and Shirley Toulson (Wildwood House)

THE PEMBROKESHIRE COAST

As usual, the HMSO guide to the park is an informative work of reference, particularly for the walker who is as much interested in flowers, birds and castles as he is in admiring the scenery. But it is not a practical guide to walking in the park. A much more attractive and readable introduction to the park is provided by the *Handbook* published by the national park committee. This describes each section of the park and contains some beautiful colour illustrations.

The national park committee publishes a booklet, *Trails in Pembrokeshire*, which describes a dozen or so short walks. These include nature trails on Skomer and near Marloes; walks around Dinas Head and St David's; and walks in the southern part of the Daugleddau near Upton Castle and Carew. The booklet refers to further leaflets describing the individual walks, most of which are published by the park committee. The Wales Tourist Board's *Wales Walking* also contains many suggestions for short walks.

For walkers, perhaps the chief feature of this national park is the coast path. Mention can be made here of the two guides to the path. Patrick Stark's little book (see page 174) offers helpful and interesting notes on the various stages of the walk and is designed to be used in conjunction with the OS 1:50,000 maps. John Barrett's HMSO guide *The Pembrokeshire Coast Path* contains 1:25,000 maps for the whole route and is therefore completely self-contained. The maps are accompanied by detailed notes on the geology and natural history of the coastline. Safe access points to the shore are shown, and there is much else of interest in this excellent book.

For those wishing to explore the Amroth to Tenby area, South Pembrokeshire District Council publishes a very commendable little booklet of short walks – *Rambles Around Tenby* – and the Friends of Saundersfoot have produced a large-scale *Saundersfoot and District Foothpath Map*.

A leaflet prepared by the Naturalists' Trust describes birdlife and other features of interest on the walk round Dinas Head, and is obtainable from the national park office.

Marloes Nature Trail*
Penally Nature Trail*
Skomer Nature Trail*
Nature Trails in Dyfed*
Rambles around Tenby*
Saundersfoot and District Footpath Map*
Slebech Forest Walk*
Trails in Pembrokeshire*
Walk Series*: Deer Park, Marloes; St David's to Caerfai; Upton Castle Grounds; Walk around Carew; Walk around St David's Head.
(All the above from the Pembrokeshire Coast National Park Office)
Handbook (Pembrokeshire National Park Committee)

SNOWDONIA

Once again, the best published guide to the national park for the walker is the OS Outdoor Leisure Map. The park is covered by five such maps, and these can be supplemented by the ½in to 1 mile map of the whole national park, which is the best available map for planning expeditions into Snowdonia. After this, the mountain walker's best guide is W. A. Poucher's *The Welsh Peaks*, which is worth obtaining for the fine photographs as much as the route descriptions. For shorter walks in lower country, the national park office has produced a number of leaflets, and there are good books by Ralph Maddern and J. T. C. Knowles (the latter having been published in the Frederick Warne Series). There is also a host of suggestions for short walks in the tourist board's booklet *Wales Walking*. Among more general publications, the HMSO guide can be recommended because it contains a long chapter by Edmund Vale entitled 'Exploring the Park', in which a number of suggestions for walks in various parts of Snowdonia are offered. Also highly recommended are William Condry's *The Snowdonia National Park* in the New Naturalist series, and Showell Styles's *The Mountains of North Wales*. The former gives an evocative description of the most interesting parts of the park; the latter is written by an eminent author who conveys better than anyone else the unique character of this majestic area.

Ralph Maddern's *Snowdonia: Ancient Trackways, Roman Roads and Packhorse Trails* describes the old highways.

Leaflets for individual waymarked trails are available in advance from the national park information officer or in the park itself at one of the several visitor centres.

The principal tracks to the summit of Snowdon itself are described in detail in leaflets specially prepared by the national park office.

Some short walks starting from stations on the Cambrian coast line have been described by Showell Styles in a booklet entitled *Public Footpath Walks from the Cambrian Coast Railway*. Styles has also written a companion booklet on walks from the stations along the private line through the Vale of Ffestiniog.

The Snowdonia National Park William Condry (Fontana)
The Mountains of North Wales Showell Styles (Gollancz)
I Bought a Mountain Thomas Firbank (Harrap)
Snowdonia: Ancient Trackways, Roman Roads and Packhorse Trails* Ralph Maddern, (Focus Publications, 9 Priors Road, Windsor, Berks SL4 4PD)
Walk in the Beautiful Conwy Valley* Ralph Maddern (Focus Publications). 12 walks.

Walk in Magnificent Snowdonia* Ralph Maddern (Focus Publications). 16 walks.

Walks for Motorists – Snowdonia (Northern Area)* J. T. C. Knowles (Frederick Warne)

Snowdonia National Park Publications* (Information Service, Snowdonia National Park):

Precipice Walk (Dolgellau)

Snowdon: Watkin Path; Pen-y-Pass; Rhyd ddu Path; Llanberis Path; Ranger Path.

Walks around Llanrwst

Walks on Cader Idris: Pony Path from Ty Nant; Minffordd Path; Pony Path from Llanfihangel y Pennant.

Walks from the Ffestiniog Railway* (Showell Styles, Borth-y-gest, Porthmadog LL49 9TW)

Public Footpath walks from the Cambrian Coast Railway* (Showell Styles)

Index

189